THE

CELEBRATION

OF

LIFE

THE
CELEBRATION
OF
LIFE

A Dialogue on Hope, Spirit,
and the
Immortality of the Soul

NORMAN COUSINS

BANTAM BOOKS
NEW YORK • TORONTO • LONDON • SYDNEY • AUCKLAND

This edition contains the complete text
of the original hardcover edition.
NOT ONE WORD HAS BEEN OMITTED.

THE CELEBRATION OF LIFE

A Bantam Book / published in association with
the Estate of Norman Cousins.

PRINTING HISTORY
Harper & Row edition published 1974
Bantam edition / August 1991

ISBN 0-553-35455-8

Published simultaneously in the United States and Canada

PRINTED IN THE UNITED STATES OF AMERICA

To my daughters,
Andrea,
Amy,
Candis,
Sarah Kit,
from whom I continue to learn,
and whose creative growth
is reassuring to a
hovering father.

Contents

Preface

This dialogue was originally presented as a philosophical statement in the Earle Lecture series at the Pacific School for Religion in Berkeley, California. William Ernest Hocking, dean of the School of Philosophy at Harvard University, was good enough to encourage publication at the time and took initiatives in that direction. I deferred publication, however, in order to test the ideas in the manuscript against the further evolution of my thought on the subject.

The dialogue has been enlarged and refined over the years, although the basic thesis and structure are unchanged. One development in particular—the ability of human beings to liberate themselves from earth gravity and to have a direct encounter with the universe—sets the general stage for this version of the dialogue.

A more precise title for this book perhaps might be "Consequentialism," which defines the central nature of the ideas in the dialogue, and which serves to position those ideas in relation to existentialism.

I have debts in many directions for this book: to William Ernest Hocking for his truly massive encouragement; to two of my teachers—William Heard Kilpatrick and Harold A. Rugg, of Teachers College, Columbia University, who never separated education from philosophy in their worldview; to Eugene Exman, who was my editor at Harper & Brothers and whose generosity of spirit and patience figured largely in the creation of this book; to Andrew Ettinger, for his initiative in bringing about the publication of this enlarged version, and for his textual suggestions; and to Leslie Meredith of Bantam, for her insightful editing. My thanks, too, to Susan Schiefelbein, Mary Swift, and Jean Anderson for their help in the preparation of the manuscript.

A Note About Style

The rebellion in recent years against the symbols of male arrogance in language is inevitable and understandable. The English language is a medium of great range and suppleness, but it has failed its users in one serious respect: It lacks the noun, pronoun, and possessive to describe both men and women.

Nothing is less gracious or more awkward, however, than the persistent use of "he or she" or "his and her" in an effort to correct the deficiency.

As used in this book, the word "man" is used only in the absence of acceptable replacements; it is not intended to elevate one half of the human race or to denigrate the other. A term like "the brotherhood of man" has philosophical and even poetic origins and need not be arbitrarily eliminated. To be sure, it is possible to substitute terms like "human beings" or "oneness," but with repeated use, they, too, can become cumbersome and clanking. "The human species" or "human beings" or variants thereof, when used repeatedly, tend to become overly grandiose and portentous.

Writers have an obligation to avoid graceless euphemisms

and inelegant language. The use of traditional nouns and pronouns in this book, therefore, is not to be interpreted as a lack of sensitivity to the need for higher linguistic standards. New terms will have to be invented. The author will be among the first to employ these terms when they appear.

THE

CELEBRATION

OF

LIFE

1

Memory
and
Continuity

One grows into one's philosophy. Year by year an individual is shaped by the sights, the sounds, the ideas around him. Consciously or not, he is forever adding to or subtracting from the sum total of his beliefs or attitudes or responses, or whatever it is we mean when we say that a person has a certain outlook on life. I do not mean to say that clearly defined truths of religions and philosophies are inevitably subject to the interpretation of an individual according to his or her experience. But I would like to suggest that one of the prime glories of the human mind is that the same idea or occurrence is never absorbed in precisely the same way by any two individuals who may be exposed to it. Each of us views a sunset, reads a book, or participates in a conversation in a different way from another, and each will take from these experiences a different meaning and memory, which will enrich the common human experience.

In this sense, each human being is a process—a filtering process of retention or rejection, absorption or loss. This process gives each person individuality. It determines whether a human being justifies the gift of human life, or whether he or she lives and dies without having been affected by the beauty of wonder, and the wonder of beauty, without having had any real awareness of kinship or human fulfillment.

Can any individual recognize and define the essence of his own individuality? Can a camera photograph itself? It can in a mirror, but even the mirror sees only the outside of the camera. A mind that attempts to perceive itself can use the tools of language and logic. But the material with which it deals is beyond mere words or reason. The marrow of human thought or personality eludes its own product—human analysis—even with the most advanced scientific instrumentation.

So, if we are to pursue our essential philosophical quest in the world—our search for integration—we need to bring together rational philosophy, spiritual belief, scientific knowledge, personal experience, and direct observation into an organic whole.

In pursuing this integration, we turn to a device worked out more than 2,300 years ago: the Socratic dialogue. The dialogue as a literary device goes back to Socrates. Its function is to provide a path for the systematic exploration of ideas. As used by the Greeks, the dialogue seemed uniquely suited to philosophical thought. The relationship of human beings not just to each other but to the universe, the ability of people to take command of historical experience, the importance attached to abstract ideas and the need to define values and to put them to work, the reach of human beings when confronted with great challenge, the contemplation of the connection between cause and effect—all these aspects of the human situation were central to the dialogue.

After 2,300 years, the matters scrutinized in the Socratic dialogue are still in the forefront of human consciousness, made all the more insistent because of the new physical connections being made by humans with the surrounding universe. The fact that the human species has been able to break out of its earth gravitational field has set the stage for vast leaps of the scientific and philosophical imagination. Perhaps the most compelling aspect of the ventures into the Solar System is the way infinity and immortality have become companion pieces in the contemplative arena.

Lending additional relevance to this conjunction is the fact that the main debates in contemporary philosophy are not so much over the nature of things as they are over the meaning of things. These debates enliven the world of creative and systematic thought and do not necessarily counterpose philosophy against science or religion. The profound advances in knowledge have not so much shrunk the unknown as they have expanded it. New questions serve mainly to enlarge old mysteries.

Socrates knew that the shortest distance between two philosophical points was a provocative question. Socrates' "questions" and observations were actually way stations to previously prepared positions. In the dialogue, the respondent does not serve as an opponent in debate or even as a full-fledged participant. Indeed, sometimes he sounds as if he were partially a forensic handyman, or alter ego. For the most part, his function is to pose the developmental questions. In this text, italics are used to indicate the respondent role.

One of the interesting characteristics of the English language is that the words that mean the most to us often lack precise meaning. Consider words or terms like "human spirit" and "soul." We are richer because of these words, yet we have difficulty in defining them.

Do we have to define them so long as we know what they mean?

No, but what is most significant about these words, perhaps, is that they are more than words; they are concepts. When we talk about the human spirit, for example, many things come to mind. What comes to your mind when I use the term?

Mostly I think it describes all those things that are beyond material limitations. It describes human beings at their best.

Good definition. The human spirit would apply, would it not. to our ability to meet great challenges? I also think of grace under pressure, especially under circumstances of ordeal or anguish. The human spirit suggests courage, of course. Also, dignity and the will to live. One thinks of William Faulkner's phrase, "the capacity to prevail." Now, what about soul? What does that mean to you?

Wouldn't it depend on who is using the word? If I heard the word "soul" in a sermon, it might mean something different from the way it would be used in a novel.

Good point. When a theologian speaks about the human soul he may be thinking about something that endures beyond one's physical presence on earth. When novelists or poets or philosophers speak of soul, they probably have in mind all the attributes that give human beings a special station in the universe. Putting it differently, the word "soul" is used to indicate that a human being is not to be regarded as an assemblage of material parts. For example, you probably recall it being said of someone, "Now, there's a person with a soul." What comes to mind is that the person being described has highly developed sensitivities, is aware of the preciousness of life, and is creatively compassionate. At the very least, it means that the person we are talking about is deserving of respect.

Our next question has to do with immortality.

Why immortality?

Only because it is the most personal matter that can engage the human mind. We can talk about the cosmos, we can talk about creation, we can talk about the nature of life, even about the nature of nature. But all this only sets the stage for the ultimate answer man seeks—which is about himself. Man may be fascinated with ultimate causes, but he is more than fascinated—he is concerned—about ultimate destination. In particular, personal destination.

Such a question is a highly personal one. I want to know whether my life is an end in itself or whether there is something beyond my life that has meaning even though I may not be able to define it.

However vague those ideas may be, they inevitably shape the entire pattern and texture of your philosophy, do they not? And thinking about immortality—at some time or other in life—is one of the great universals of human experience. Julian Huxley, the eminent biologist and philosopher, once said that the highest aspirations of mankind—which we might suggest are our quests for understanding ourselves, our world, our fellow human beings, and for dealing with all with integrity—lead to a doctrine of immortality.

Would you agree that there is no standardization in man's thinking about immortality? That concepts of immortality, like concepts of art and beauty, vary from culture to culture, and, indeed, from person to person?

That stands to reason.

But though concepts of immortality may differ, the quest that underlies the concepts is substantially the same. And we can attempt to define the nature of this quest for purposes of our discussion.

That would be helpful.

Shall we say, then, that most persons in the course of history have longed for immortality, and that this desire is expressed in various beliefs or philosophical speculations?

That approach is acceptable. I observe, however, that you used the expression "most persons." Isn't the longing for immortality universal?

A good point. The longing for immortality is as nearly universal as anything we know pertaining to the inner wishes of human beings; but some, from time to time, have renounced any interest in the subject of immortality. They are lost, however, in the actual day-to-day quest for immortality. So much so that we can strengthen our earlier definition, if you wish, by saying that the quest for immortality may actually reflect the inherent desire in human beings for the indefinite perpetuation of self.

Isn't this the same thing as defining immortality?

Only in a general way. What most concepts of immortality have in common is the belief in continued spirit or substance or both. The individual expects to retain continuity, certainly to retain memory, from this world to the next—at least to the extent of having a full awareness of what he was in this world. But, may I ask if you can regard immortality in other than purely personal terms?

I don't follow the question. When we began a moment ago, you said there was nothing more personal than the subject of immortality. Now you are asking me if I can take a less personal view of it.

My question has to do not with the meaning immortality holds for you, but rather with your method of considering it. To be specific, can you conceive of immortality without continuity of personal memory?

When you speak of "personal memory," you refer to my full awareness in a future state of who I was in my past life—which is to say, this life?

Yes.

And you want to know if I can conceive of an immortality without conscious connection to my life in this world.

Yes.

My answer would have to be "no." How can I be expected to contemplate the meaning of immortality if my immortal self would not know who my mortal self was? If I am deprived of continuity of memory, how would I know I was immortal? Obviously, I would have to know later who I am now. And I want to know now that I shall know this later.

So that if you are to find meaning in anything, you must retain some connection with your own experience?

Isn't it natural for me to want to do this?

It is natural enough; I am merely asking if you would be willing for the moment to consider an immortality in which the personal factor would not be predominant.

That seems to be a contradiction in terms. The moment the personal factor ceases to be predominant, we are not talking about immortality, but about something else.

But suppose a higher immortality is actually possible.

A higher kind of immortality?

What I am trying to get you to agree to—for the moment, at least—is that a higher immortality may actually be of a kind in which your own place in it might be as something other than the personal you.

Are you referring now to Hindu belief that I may be reborn in another life-form?

No. Let me approach immortality from an entirely different vantage point. Suppose you were to lose all memory of past events, perhaps as the result of an accident. You would want to continue to exist, would you not, assuming you were otherwise injured?

Yes, I would want to live.

You agree, then, that consciousness is so precious, and human life so desirable, that you would want to go on living even though you felt that you had no direct memory connection with what had happened before your accident?

Certainly. There is much more to life than memory. There is the enjoyment of living; there is life itself.

If, therefore, you see an even more vital connection with life itself than with personal memory, wouldn't you accept the concept of a hereafter in which you would have a part even though you would have no knowledge of who you had been in this life?

I don't suppose I would rule it out.

Then, if existence or consciousness is desirable, you would welcome it, would you not, even if you had no memory continuity?

I don't know. You confuse me.

Aren't you confused because our thinking has been so tied to the idea of a thoroughly personal immortality that we are unwilling to accept any other kind? Apart from the question of whether a hereafter is worthwhile without personal memory, can you conceive that a hereafter is possible on a less egotistical basis?

I suppose so. But what good would such a hereafter do me?

What is it you expect in the hereafter? Do you crave pleasure?

I certainly don't anticipate pain.

Do you crave great honors in the hereafter?

I don't think so.

Do you crave heroic deeds, wisdom, riches, health? Exactly what do you expect, what do you ask, of the hereafter?

Well, I am not quite sure. I suppose all I expect is peace of mind. I want to be saved from an eternity in death.

But beyond the fact that the idea of death is repugnant, you have no specific ideas as to what you expect beyond life?

No, I suppose not.

Isn't non-death a rather limited idea? Shouldn't your quest for immortality involve more than the mere desire to avoid a shattering blow to your conceit?

It ought to; but it doesn't seem an easy thing to wish for.

If you were searching for life without design merely to escape from the discontinuation of self, then surely you must recognize that such escape is the result of the excessive claims of an unreasonable ego?

I guess so. But what about my soul?

Let's return for a moment to the ideas we opened our dialogue with. We had decided that spirit and soul were words for a non-material manifestation of self. Would you still agree?

Yes.

Then, you are saying, are you not, that the soul is higher than the ego—at least, that it is above the petty limitations of ego?

Yes.

If the soul is above the excessive demands of the ego, then it would make no difference to the soul whether or not there is continuity of personal memory.

That would follow.

Therefore, we ought not to cater to the ego's insistence on personal memory as the essential ingredient of immortality. If the soul or spirit is immortal in an entirely different sense, it may, in fact, represent a much higher form of immortality than the conventional one.

I begin to see your point.

Since you are now willing to make a distinction between soul and ego, placing the former ahead of the latter, are you also willing to accept the concept of soul without personal memory?

Do I have a choice?

Not in the ultimate sense, perhaps, but aren't you at least entitled now to the peace of mind that comes from knowing that immortality may be possible and desirable without continuity of personal memory?

I agree now that it may be possible. But you also used the word "desirable." Why is it desirable?

Why must immortality cease to be worthwhile the moment human conceit is defeated? If immortality is desirable with memory, would it be any less desirable without it so long as the soul is fulfilled?

In that sense, yes, I agree. It would be desirable.

We have now reached the point, therefore, where you agree that you are willing to liberate yourself from one aspect of the usual concept of immortality, which is to say, perpetuation of the ego self. Are you willing to consider other aspects of immortality?

Yes.

Let us proceed to the time aspect of immortality. How long does immortality last?

That's easy; immortality lasts forever.

Suppose immortality did not last quite that long, but long enough. Would you reject it on that score?

How long is long enough?

Suppose immortality for you would stretch ahead only as long as the combined years of every human being who ever lived; suppose that you had 10,000 billion years of hereafter. Would you reject immortality on the grounds that that was not long enough?

Well, once we put any limit on immortality, it ceases to be immortality. Still, 10,000 billion years is a long time.

You would not reject it, then?

No, I would not reject it on that score. But I don't know why you selected that number.

That number is purely hypothetical. As a rough guess, it represents the total number of years lived by every person since our emergence as human beings. If you feel a direct biological and spiritual connection with every human being who has ever lived—if you can conceive of the immortality of the bloodstream or of the human spirit—then you are already in possession of at least 10,000 billion years of immortality. And if you can make the great identification with every human being now alive or who is to live, there is the prospect of many more billions of years ahead.

As you describe it, you make me think that this is almost too much accumulated immortality for one person to bear.

Very well, then, let's make it less astronomical. If the human race has existed for 600,000 years in its present form, then your genes or your bloodstream or whatever it is that represents the "renewable you" has in fact been in existence for that length of time.

Yes, I follow that. In fact, I almost prefer the smaller figure. It somehow makes it seem more intimate.

You agree, then, that the proof of your immortality is in the fact of your own existence? Descartes saw proof of existence in thought. He might also have said, "I exist, therefore I am immortal." For the "personal you" is periodic and evanescent; the "renewable you" is eternal and immortal, at least to the extent that the human bloodstream or human spirit itself is immortal. I use bloodstream in the symbolic sense; technically, of course, we are talking about genes. The only remaining question is whether the human being is capable of recognizing this bloodstream as the headwaters of his immortality. Nothing is really elusive about immortality except our comprehension of it.

You mean that the answer lies in the imagination?

Yes, if by the imagination you would also include the ability of we human beings to raise prodigiously the threshold of our awareness so that we see ourselves for what we really are: individual cells, in the immortal body of humanity. Need we torment ourselves with questions of personal immortality if we can recognize the concept of a higher immortality?

I guess not.

A moment ago you referred to the imagination. This gift of imagination, combined with knowledge, enables you to do more than participate only theoretically in the lives of those who have lived before you. Through the art of creative reading, for example, the panorama of history can be spread before you. The grand individual experiences in history can be reborn and fulfilled in your imagination. The past is dead only for those who lack the gift to bring it to life. As you think about immortality, need you confine it to the future? Shouldn't you include the past and thus regard yourself as beneficiary of immortality in reverse? Today is the hereafter of yesterday's here-and-now.

Now I see what you meant when you said earlier that I could find proof of immortality in my very existence.

May I ask now if you see any connection between what we have been talking about and spiritual ethics?

I am not sure I do.

Wouldn't it follow, from what we have discussed, that the higher immortality depends on an inspired acceptance of the concept of humankind's interrelationship and interdependency? Isn't the essence of immortality the familial interconnectedness of humanity?

I think I see this, but I am not sure.

If we can truly comprehend the reality of the family of humanity and our places in it, if we truly regard the human bloodstream as the source and proof of our immortality, won't we thereby be prepared to comprehend what we have called the higher immortality? Isn't recognition of the reality of human commonality the prerequisite for this elevated threshold of awareness—awareness that can perceive a higher immortality?

So there is no real loss if there is no continuity of personal memory?

That is the heart of the matter. The very absence of personal memory constitutes the essence of that which is desirable in a higher immortality. Isn't the immortality of the species or of the human spirit a richer and deeper concept than the more limited form of personal immortality?

Yes, that would stand to reason.

Then, you agree that the pathway to a realizable immortality, as I said a moment ago, is the idea of true human oneness?

But I am troubled. Must we wait until such true oneness exists before we can realize a higher immortality?

No. The fact of humankind exists. However, the general recognition of such a brotherhood does not exist. Humankindness ought to be central in all our thinking, but it is not. Nor does it yet serve as the basis for our day-to-day actions or our philosophies or our behavior as nations—but this does not change our basic oneness of human spirit. Imperfect knowledge of oneself and one's fellow humans stems from not recognizing this oneness.

Are there other implications?

THE CELEBRATION OF LIFE

The implications are endless. One of them most certainly is that immortality is a living reality. As we observed a moment ago, immortality is a product not of the hereafter but of the here-and-now, the fulfillment of which, as we have seen, is directly tied to total awareness of the meaning of human commonality. You live in others; others live in you. So long as any human being lives, you have life. Therefore, your passport to immortality, to be valid, must have the stamp of the human community upon it.

2

The World in Our Mirror

Before proceeding, let us see how far we have come. You have now made some modifications in your original approach to the question or concept of immortality and the soul.

That is right.

First, you modified the demands of the ego—the continuity of memory. Second, you enlarged your concept of immortality from only a future lifetime to one that includes past lifetimes that find fulfillment in you. Thus we formed an idea of what we might call "achieved or interim immortality": in your being you embody the immortality of those who preceded you. In turn, you are embodied in the immortality of those who follow. Then in our discussion we came to the need for a living philosophy based on a humankindness, a spirit that has an organic connection with a higher immortality.

I am still bothered by one thing. I can now conceive of immortality in higher, or at least different, terms. I was able to divorce my personal substance and memory from my contemplation of what happens after death. But your point about "achieved immortality" and human oneness connects me with physical substance in the sense that it connects me with people. Isn't this a contradiction? Doesn't any connection with physical substance tend to weaken the concept of a higher immortality?

Not necessarily. I was hopeful that I might persuade you that by projecting your personal pride to pride in the human family, you might derive proper satisfaction from the fact that your essence has been alive half a million years or more and will probably continue to be alive a lot longer.

And what about my spirit?

Your spirit is a manifestation of your essence—and vice versa. There are no limits to the nature or meaning of the human spirit except your own comprehension of it. The more elevated your comprehension of the human spirit, the greater your pride in being part of it—yesterday, today, tomorrow.

You are restoring my ego.

I didn't mean to shatter it—merely to try to put it in a somewhat larger setting. The need is not to amputate the ego but to transcend it.

Why must it be necessary to transcend the ego? What is there so wrong with the ego in the first place? You almost make it sound like a dangerous vestigial structure—as though it were an appendix of the psyche that has to be removed lest it do fatal damage.

The comparison of the ego with the appendix is not entirely apt, although the ego can become dangerous when inflamed—to the individual and to society. Unlike the appendix, however, the human ego is necessary. It is the basis of personal achievement. It is a fundamental resource of human progress. We need to be recognized; we need to be known by our good works; we need to be loved.

In all these respects, the ego is important and indispensable. The concept of human brotherhood would be impossible without it, for no one can truly know love for others unless he or she can respond to it. But if the ego governs absolutely, then an individual loses his or her vital balance and is ruled solely by personal tastes and needs—and becomes hostile to his or her own nature. The human higher self is to be found in our identification with our fellow humans. An unbridled ego will destroy the harmony on which our emotional well-being depends. So, we need to transcend the ego. And when we do this, we are satisfied in different, certainly more fundamental, ways. In fact, you might almost say your satisfactions are reversed.

Reversing my satisfactions? What does that mean?

As you begin to shape your life on the working acceptance of human brotherhood, your ego becomes less and less dictatorial and unreasonable. And when the concept of human brotherhood takes on the dimension for you of a living reality, you will have succeeded in liberating yourself completely from the tyranny of the ego.

Such a liberation can do strange and wonderful things to your expectations and satisfactions. You will derive your supreme satisfaction not from your ability to amass things or to achieve superficial power but from your ability to identify yourselves with others and to share fully in their needs and hopes. In short, for fulfillment, we look to identification rather than acquisition.

This sounds fine in theory, but I am not sure I see it as a working reality. It takes two to share something. If you regard the next person as a brother, but your "brother" does not accept that honor, how do you go about advancing the concept? Haven't some of our longest and bloodiest wars come about because some people happened to get the notion that other people ought to be their brothers whether they liked it or not? Isn't it just a short step from regarding yourself as someone's brother to regarding yourself as your brother's keeper?

There is an important distinction to be made between a fundamental belief in human kinship and the philosophy that you are your brother's keeper. I use the word "keeper" in the sense in which it was originally implied—namely, a combination of overseer and guardian. It is one thing to say that part of you comes to life in other human beings and that you are therefore affected by their hurts or their needs or their moral splendor, and quite another thing to say that you are their appointed guardian. In the former case you are fulfilling your true nature. In the latter case, you are not transcending your ego, but are only stretching it.

I can accept this. I can see the distinction between a sense of human oneness and the distorted idea that one must direct another person's fate. But, as I asked a moment ago, I still wonder whether it isn't too easy to erase the narrow line that separates the two. How do we go about pursuing the concept of a human family without inevitably coming into conflict with members of that family?

A good point. As you said earlier, some of the bloodiest wars in history have been carried on in the name of brotherly love. We can think of dozens of instances of swords being drawn to drive home the point of eternal friendship and even salvation. Good impulses and good concepts can be distorted, but this is no argument for their elimination. Water can choke you if you swallow it the wrong way, but this is no argument against water. Certainly it is possible for a person to make the great identification with others without attempting to dominate them. In fact, the identification is false if there is any will to dominate. If the identification is real, then there is no desire in one person to harm another. Rather, a person will think in terms of mutual growth and respect and will do whatever possible to create the conditions in which such mutuality is possible. This mutuality affords satisfactions far deeper than those usually fed to the ego.

But isn't competition a law of life?

If by competition we are thinking of a certain zest for life, a desire to do one's best according to the rules of the game, and a respect for the other person's chances under the same rules, then such behavior is a healthy outlet for human competitive characteristics. But if by competitiveness you mean the rule of the jungle in human affairs, then we are doomed, for it is only a question of time before our combative skills and weapons reach the point of absolute annihilation.

I will rephrase my question: Isn't combative competitiveness a basic law of life?

No responsible anthropologist of whom I am aware has made that statement. Quite the opposite: the anthropologist knows the human species to be infinitely malleable with a profound capacity for making adjustments related to survival. And as soon as enough humans understand that the conditions of survival today require a greater sense and spirit of mutuality than ever before, we are apt to experience some of the strongest and most important changes in history.

Is there any real chance that humanity will actually convince itself of the need for fundamental change?

I don't think I said that there is a need for a change in the fundamental nature of humans. The words I used were intended to refer to what are supposed to be predominantly competitive characteristics. But there is just as much evidence to indicate that humans respond to kinship or sacrifice or love as much as we do to the competitive side of our nature. In any event, we do not have to go against our basic nature in subduing jungle habits or responses. We have merely to assert what already exists deep within us—namely, a sense of kinship.

Are you saying that we fulfill our nature when we live out the idea of human kinship?

Nothing is more basic in human nature than the profound capacity to find satisfaction in compassion and identification. We have heard a great deal about the tensions and pressures that build up inside us when we fail to find an outlet for our aggressive drives. But it is also true that we humans suffer great uneasiness when we fail to find an outlet for our natural goodness. When we are blocked from identifying with one another, when we are cut off from the larger part of ourselves—humankind—we develop all sorts of troubles of the psyche; we become neurotic. Our happiness depends on being in touch with ourselves through our oneness with others.

Must I sacrifice in order to be happy?

"Sacrifice" is a big word. Let us say "identify" in a way that would include sacrifice but not limit it to that. And the business of identification works both ways. There are no limits to our ability to respond to appeals made to our natural goodness, just as we have an enormous capacity for responding to sacrifices made by others for us. In fact, it is doubtful whether there is any greater power in human affairs than that exerted through the example of love for others.

What specific examples are you thinking of?

All the world's great spiritual leaders have derived their power largely by making the supreme identification—namely, by offering their lives in the cause of human need or ennoblement. When we study the lives of these leaders, we see that each of them was aware that the example of renunciation and sacrifice awakens powerful forces in human beings.

Christianity would not have existed without the Crucifixion. The conviction that Jesus gave his life not for an abstract cause but for every person who ever lived or was to live is at the heart of Christian belief. The true Christian is not one who merely affiliates, but one who feels Christ and the ideas of Jesus as an inner reality. And true feeling is not necessarily the same as glorified rote.

What do you mean by "glorified rote"?

Simply the elaborate recitation of Jesus' ideas without any real feeling for their relevance or practicality in human affairs. How many people do you know who believe in the Sermon on the Mount as a working guide to everyday living, as a charter for society, as a mandate in world affairs? How many political representatives would accept its validity as a strict basis for national decision?

When you put it that way, I find it difficult to come up with any specific names.

Yet the principal significance of Christianity is to be found not in terms of mechanical acceptance, but in the fact of its essential appeal. That is why the life of Jesus, what he said, what he did, and the way he died, awakens such powerful responses in people. He believed, literally, in the kinship of humanity and therefore represents the quintessence of the higher immortality we have been talking about. Jesus didn't speak for Christianity; Jesus spoke for the individual. Incidentally, we must never forget that Jesus spoke as a Jew. He asserted his Hebrew faith. He sought to reform Judaism, not to depart from it. And Jesus always put his emphasis on the individual person. In fact, all the world's truly great spiritual leaders have spoken for the individual human being, rather than for any designated group or class. And they all awakened powerful responses through the example of their own identification and sacrifice.

But what about Buddha and Confucius and Muhammad? There was no spectacular personal sacrifice in their experiences, was there? No

*one of the three derived his influence from the fact that he gave his life
for the cause of individual man. Each of these Eastern religious leaders
lived a full life and died a natural death. Yet the total number of people
who have accepted their ideas or faith is many times greater than the
number of those who have followed Western religions. Doesn't this refute
your idea that the great religious leaders made their appeals through total
identification, dramatized by the circumstances of their death or suffering?*

These are interesting questions. First of all, though, it may
be useful to ask whether you are willing to reconsider one statement
you just made that seemed to put your questions in a certain context,
and I am not sure that that context is correct.

What statement of mine do you have in mind?

You referred to Eastern religions and Western religions in
a way that would seem to indicate that you were dealing with clearly
recognizable and separate entities. And then you juxtaposed each
against the other, as though they were almost contradictory.

Is there anything so wrong with that?

It is a serious error—though a common one. If you are
considering this purely from the geographical standpoint, you might
begin with the fact that Christianity may number most of its prac-
titioners in the West, but it originated in the East and is certainly
no less Eastern than the Islamic faith in content. Jesus Christ was
an Asian. So was Paul. Christianity became a Western religion
purely by adoption and not by origin. Judaism, which is a substantial
part of the religious heritage of the West, is equally Eastern.

Within the Eastern religions themselves, there are important differences between Islam and Hinduism, between Buddhism and Confucianism, between Shintoism and Bahaism. It is impossible to fashion a single generalization that would justify placing them all in a single category in contrast to Western religions.

I am willing to make some modification of my earlier question, then, that will take all this into account. Yet I cannot help wondering whether you don't recognize at least some fundamental differences between Eastern and Western thought. Surely, the expressions "Judeo-Christian tradition" and "Eastern mysticism" have been used so frequently that they must mean something quite specific.

In the minds of the users, perhaps. But there is very little real substance behind those expressions.

Are there any generalizations about East and West that are sanctioned by good scholarship?

One wonders. I suppose, though, if you look at the East with respect to its component parts, and then do the same for the West, each of the parts might warrant some generalizations. Only when the generalizations are applied to a nonexistent whole do we get into trouble.

What generalizations can be made about the parts?

Well, we can generalize, for example, about the origins of Greek thought by saying that there was an early tradition in Greek thinking that was concerned about man's place in the world around him and his approach to that world. We can generalize about Hindu thought by saying that it is an attempt to deal with the comprehensive totality of an individual's existence. We can generalize about Confucian thought by saying that it is concerned about man's relationship to his fellow man, what the rules of the good life are, and what one's obligations to his family are, and how important it is for these relationships to have spiritual significance.

Perhaps the largest generalization of all that we can make is that whatever the differences in doctrine, dogma, pure theology, there is a common recognition of the power of human conscience. In India, it took the form of release from suffering through penance and renunciation. In Islam, it took the form of detachment of self for the cause of union with God. In Greece, it took the form of intellectual and logical pursuit of the good and rejection of the evil.

What emerges from all this is the fact that the designations "East" and "West" as fully separate and distinct compartments are the relics of an outmoded scholarship. There is too much variety within each of the great geographical entities to warrant the use of those terms for cultural or philosophical designations.

Now, having come this far, we can return to your earlier question about the necessity of renunciation and sacrifice as a manifestation of the higher immortality. Buddha and Muhammad died normally and not in a dramatic and symbolic manner, as Jesus did. Buddha and Muhammad have much in common, at least with respect to their backgrounds. Both came of wealthy families. Both tried to see the world whole. Both recognized the need for personal renunciation.

Buddha very early in life became oppressed by the fact of human suffering and by the lack of true spirituality in the people around him. He renounced his wealth and began to talk of his spiritual beliefs, one of the tenets of which is that we cannot truly know another person unless we can share in the other's suffering.

He preached the doctrine of human kinship, saying that happiness is not to be found by oneself or for oneself, but only through identification. He believed that a person has the obligation to develop all one's capacities—physical, intellectual, spiritual, emotional—not for such satisfaction as they might provide, but because in this way one is of greatest service to one's family on earth. This idea of kinship through dedicated service and understanding, according to Buddhism, produces the only true happiness. Anyone brought up in the Judeo-Christian tradition would find nothing alien in this aspect of Buddhism.

Muhammad's real influence stems from the time he rose from a battlefield after having been given up for dead. And Muhammad's example of selflessness and his castigation of the rich for their oppression of the poor were basic in building the Islam faith. In any event, it is important to recognize the organic connection between the Koran and the Old and New Testaments. Islam is not a repudiation of most basic Judeo-Christian beliefs but a development of them. The Muslim recognizes the Ten Commandments as the basis of law; indeed, a large part of the Koran is an enlargement and particularization of these principles. The idea that the Islam faith is something totally unrelated to Western spiritual thought is inaccurate and unfortunate.

Stranger still, in fact, is the psychological gulf between Christian and Jew. Full weight has yet to be attached to the fact that Christianity, strictly speaking, is another word for Hebrew fundamentalism. It was born out of literal interpretation of Hebrew prophecy. Thus, the Hebrew religion ought not to be considered apart from Christianity, because it gave birth to it. In Judaism, the power of sacrifice and identification and the need to triumph over individual desires were clearly recognized by the prophets who stressed human kinship under the Fatherhood of God. Christianity stands firmly on this spiritual legacy. The Hebrew faith taught us that man is one because God is one. We see, therefore, that if man is one, the higher immortality is real.

What about the other religions?

In the other great religions, we can observe certain impressive universals which in the past have been subordinate to their differences but which today are important as the common element of increased world understanding. Bahā' Allāh, for example, who founded the Baha'i faith, appealed to the oneness of humanity and to the sense of human family inherent in all people. He believed that unity ought not to become solely a spiritual concept but all-pervasive in human thought and action. The test of spiritual doctrine was in its application to every aspect of life and government. Bahā' Allāh anticipated the implications of modern destructive science when he advocated world political unity.

The Hindu faith is built on universality; it regards itself as a composite arena for all religions; it knows the power of symbolic sacrifice. It sees a grand continuity of the human assemblage.

The main point in what I have just said, of course, is that the basic unity of humanity finds reflection in the basic unity of the great religions. This universality, fully felt, can be a powerful stimulus to the reality of human kinship.

Aren't examples of dedication, identification, and sacrifice apparent outside of religion?

Certainly. Socrates was the moral man whose hold on history proceeds out of the fact of his death. His death enabled him to become a living symbol for those who would war against ideas. A unifying thread that runs through the great religions and the great ideas is this appeal to the human faculty for sharing and for mutuality of sacrifice.

Is this what is meant by humanity's moral capacity?

In a large sense, yes. As I indicated a moment ago, the dividing line between religious and secular leaders is not too sharp. All the truly great persons have had some spiritual appeal. For example, how would you classify Gandhi?

Isn't he a purely political figure?

Far from it. Gandhi was concerned with political objectives, to be sure; but his appeal went far beyond politics. In fact, in years to come, Gandhi may be regarded as the most important religious figure in the twentieth century. Gandhi was willing to make the ultimate sacrifice for a moral principle. He was no less willing to sacrifice himself for a single person. The secret of his appeal lay in renunciation. And because he was able to feel this supreme identification with his fellow human beings, he exerted a greater force on history than millions of armed men on the march.

And the identification was reciprocal. People suffered when Gandhi suffered. They rejoiced in his triumphs. The British could not cope with him. They could cope with riots; they were prepared to deal with force. But in order to deal with the moral power of Gandhi, they needed a bigger moral idea, which they did not have. The point here, however, is that Gandhi appealed to that which is natural in humankind—our moral grandeur—and the people found fulfillment in their response to it and to him.

In our time we have known yet another man who was able

to awaken powerful responses in people through the power of his dedication and sacrifice. It is unimportant whether we call him a great religious figure or a great moral figure, for Albert Schweitzer's words and works are known and he was loved and has influenced others because of the power of his example. Schweitzer has been criticized as an escapist. He has been accused of patronizing the people he chose to serve. Yet the proof of Schweitzer's genuineness and his integrity is to be found in the response he awakened in people. He inspired countless millions who were able to identify themselves with him only because of the visible and splendid fact of his own identification with them. Here, too, the essential point is that brotherhood is not a mere intellectual concept but an organic part of man's nature that has only to be invoked in order to become manifest.

But we can't all become Gandhis or Schweitzers. We are merely human beings.

Did you say "merely human"? There are no "mere" humans. Moral splendor comes with the gift of life. Each person has within him or her a vast potential for identification, dedication, sacrifice, mutuality. Each person has unlimited strength to feel human oneness and act upon it. If the use of this strength is genuine, the power will make itself felt.

We may have no jurisdiction over the fact of our existence, but we are not barred from imparting meaning to that existence.

The tragedy of life is not in the fact of death, but in what dies inside a person while he or she lives.

No person need fear death; we need fear only that we may die without having known our greatest power—the power of our free will to give of our life to others. If something comes to life in others because of you, then you have made an approach to immortality.

Your mention of immortality at this point brings our discussion full circle, does it not?

We began by considering our characteristically human search for immortality, then recognized human kinship as the predominating fact of human existence. We tried to show that we need not compartmentalize our concept of immortality, and that there is a basis for complete integration among all the prime elements of our thought and action and being, involving spiritual and philosophical belief, scientific progress and political objectives, and ethics.

But there is perhaps an aspect to our discussion that so far we have not sufficiently considered.

What is that?

If your ideas live in others, then you have indeed made a contribution to the immortality of the human spirit. Or if an idea lives in you that was born in others, you are benefiting from a grand continuity of the human spirit. Of course, ideas can be good or bad.

Doesn't this create serious problems?

Any aspect of dualism in people creates problems. Whether we are talking about good versus evil, or altruism versus selfishness, or cooperativeness versus competitiveness, or cowardice versus courage, we must recognize that these very opposites represent the life-force. But it is also part of our uniqueness that we are endowed with the faculty of choice. We are not entirely helpless in the eternal struggle between good and evil that exists both inside and outside ourselves, but especially inside ourselves. If we make the right choices, then an element of progress has come into the world. In fact, progress may be just another way of saying that enough people have chosen wisely between good and evil and that these decisions have had their effects.

The moral person isn't necessarily one who has never experienced the struggle between good and evil. The moral person is one who recognizes the existence of such a struggle and does not shrink from it.

Is this the only test of individual morality?

Not entirely. If you are looking for a single yardstick by which to measure a moral person, you might say that the moral person regards the total well-being of the world, or the lack of such well-being, as flowing out of his or her own integrity and conscience, or the lack of it. This doesn't mean that he or she has responsibility for everything that happens in the world; it means that what he or she thinks and does has consequences that extend to all other people. In this sense, the moral person finds the world in his or her mirror.

3

Existentialism
and
Individualism

Would you say we are moving in our discussion toward a unified or integrated concept of ethics, religion, philosophy, and science? Also, that the closer we approach such an integrated concept, the stronger is the philosophical basis for human kinship?

I am aware that we have discussed spiritual ethics and immortality in a way that would embrace some aspects of religion, or at least of spiritual belief, and also that this line of reasoning contains a general philosophical underpinning, but I was not aware that science supports the poetic assertion of the oneness of humanity.

Only indirectly. As it concerns the human family, it is a scientific fact that no person is further removed from any other person on this earth than by fifty cousins. When mathematicians and anthropologists go back generation after generation, constructing and connecting all the genealogical lines, they contend that all persons now alive are fiftieth cousins at most.

You mean that it is more accurate to say that all people are cousins than to say that all are brothers or sisters?

Brothers, sisters, or cousins, it is all the same. We share a common origin and destiny. This doesn't mean that individuality has no value, or that diversity is not desirable. Individuality is the essence of human existence. But this doesn't change the fact that human life has common sources and is confronted by common problems and common needs. Nor does it alter the ultimate question of human destiny—a destiny in which we can retain individuality and yet be held together.

I follow that reasoning.

Would you also say that one cannot agree with these ideas without having it affect one's views of one's own life, whether with respect to everyday dealings with other people, or participation in the affairs of groups, all the way from the family to the nation and the human community itself? Integration is a basic law of life; when we resist it, disintegration is the natural result, both outside and inside us. Thus we come to the concept of harmony through integration.

When you say that we must integrate ourselves with our total environment, what about our relationship to the universe itself?

The same holds true. At one time, integration on this level was contemplative rather than participative—which is to say, the individual tried to comprehend the lines of consistency between moral order and universal order. With space exploration, however, the individual human being has a direct access to, and perception of, the cosmos.

I am glad to hear you mention the individual now and then. It seemed to me a little while ago that we were reaching back to the beginning of time and forward to the tip of eternity, but the place the individual has in our exploration wasn't too clear.

Everything that has been discussed up until now points straight to that very question. Belief in a higher immortality can be more than a mere exercise in speculative philosophy. It can be a design for living. It can help govern your life, your relationships with other people, your attitudes, your place in the political community and in the world itself. Each one of us has a special obligation to our own moment in history. Perhaps we might examine the nature of the obligation.

Certainly.

What would you say it is that our own time needs the most?

We need many things. We need peace; we need freedom; we need food; we need progress; we need an unpoisoned world.

Don't we also need a certain way of thinking about progress if we are to achieve it? What about the climate or mood in which we perceive our needs?

I would say the mood is mixed.

You are right; the world is too large an arena for any single mood. But have you also sensed the fact that there is too much negation in the general mixture? Almost everywhere you look, ideas hostile to the human potential are springing up. These ideas are defeatist. They enfeeble the human family by taking away our tomorrow. They scorn hope and they kill purpose. They are cold, impersonal. The future is difficult enough without depriving us of our will to endure, to sustain and be sustained.

In any case, the vast increase of new knowledge—and therefore of problems—has not produced new philosophies that speak uniquely to a new condition in human affairs in which we have a direct encounter with the universe.

Isn't it the primary obligation of philosophy to avoid becoming trapped in a contemporary setting?

You make a basic point. Philosophy seeks to make connections in the human mind between the memories of the race and ways of thinking about life. It constructs principles for asking meaningful questions and for disciplining the speculations those questions produce. But the test of philosophy is its ability to contribute to its own time while remaining independent of it.

When you say that the problems of the twentieth century have not generated specific and systematic philosophies for thinking about new conditions in human affairs, aren't you overlooking existentialism?

Existentialism doesn't profess to be a systematic philosophy. It is more a way of responding to historical and contemporary forces and to society than it is a coherent set of ideas. Moreover, there are so many interpretations and variants of existentialism that it is difficult to describe it with any single definition. It is important to note, however, that existentialism is primarily the creation of a nineteenth-century thinker, Søren Kierkegaard, of Denmark. Not until the early part of the twentieth century, however, did Kierkegaard's ideas make a substantial impact—not in Denmark but in Germany, a natural consequence considering the economic and political chaos that followed Germany's defeat in World War I.

Germany was not the only country experiencing chaos after that war. Why did existentialism have special meaning for Germans?

The end of that war produced a pronounced pendulum swing in Germany from a widely held sense of national omnipotence to a sense of national failure and emptiness. Various German intellectuals took up the existentialist idea that an individual's first obligation is to maintain a circle of sanity, responsibility, and awareness around his own existence. Life was surrounded by dread, yet the individual could protect himself against intellectual, spiritual, and physical paralysis. He could be guarded in his commitments. Even if his choices were limited, even if he could have no confidence that his choices might be correct, he had the obligation to live out his life and to extract from it what he could. His connections with, and obligations to, his fellow human beings were important facts of his existence but not necessarily the overriding facts. What was predominant was his need to survive in an unpredictable, harsh, and not very controllable world. He "does not know a way out," Paul Tillich has written, "but he reacts with the courage of despair." That is, he "takes his despair upon himself."

I had always associated existentialism with the early years in France following World War II—in particular with Jean-Paul Sartre and Albert Camus.

Just as it is understandable that existentialist thought took hold in Germany after World War I, so it is equally understandable that existentialism figured prominently in the intellectual climate of France after World War II. The course of the war provided little support for philosophical idealism or for positive ideas celebrating human purpose. Yet French literary figures such as Sartre and Camus, even though both were reluctant at times to define themselves as formal existentialists, responded to the general intellectual mood of disillusion and despair in much the same way that Heidegger and Jaspers had responded in Germany. The mood that emerged from their books and plays was bleak, but the human spirit was sustained nonetheless. The individual was not justified in turning away from the reality of his own existence, even though his efforts to protect it were probably doomed.

This, then, was the curious mixture of existentialism at the end of the two world wars—a compound of limited aspiration, despair, dread, and a sense of the individual's obligation to himself ahead of the collective mechanism called society.

Why didn't existentialism have the same appeal in other countries?

The interest in existentialism was considerable, especially as modified affirmatively by later writers, notably Paul Tillich and Teilhard de Chardin. But it did not completely satisfy those whose history had not taken them to a dead end. For people who believed that historical logic supported the idea of a positive frame for human events, existentialism lacked dynamic thrust. True, it didn't present itself as a philosophy of resignation, but that seemed to be its effect. By accommodating itself to helplessness and hopelessness, existentialism fostered the very mood of negation it originally sought to dispel. It runs contrary to human history to say there is "No Exit," as Sartre did in the title of one of his plays.

You referred earlier to Tillich's idea of a "courageous despair."

Existentialism did great honor to the concept of human individuality and to the things that belong to the individual and not to society. If it appeared to sanction cynicism, it also fortified and enlivened the philosophical process, one reflection of which is the diversification of existentialism itself. It also had a world impact— far greater, perhaps, than the pragmatic philosophy of William James or the earlier affirmative philosophy of the American transcendentalists.

In the main, however, existentialism has not been an effective or appropriate response for the present human condition and the predicament it has been unable to resolve: the human species possesses the means to expunge itself but lacks a broad understanding of the unifying ideas for safeguarding and ennobling its future. Nor is existentialism an antidote to the growing feeling of helplessness and hopelessness among individual human beings all over the world. Quite the contrary, what ties most existentialists together is precisely this feeling of helplessness—helplessness to shape the collective destiny, helplessness to preside over erratic and painful events, helplessness in recognizing and facing up to anguishing choices.

If the helplessness is predicated on reality, doesn't it have validity?

The ability of the human species to do that which has never been done before demonstrates the greatest of all historical truths. The notion of individual helplessness is therefore unhistoric and unnatural. It is a notion that has gained currency at certain times, of which the present is an example. What generally happens is that supposedly inexorable forces gather strength in combination with personalized malevolence. At such times, enough evil is inflicted on enough people to produce a lowering ceiling over human hopes. The result is that the individual becomes spiritually devitalized and despairing.

How do notions of helplessness and hopelessness arise?

Notions of helplessness in our time stem from at least four main causes. One cause is represented by the collective sense of an imminent self-inflicted defeat. The particulars are familiar: Population is swelling, but the food supply is shrinking. Energy needs are growing faster than new sources of energy can be generated or developed. Oxygen is being depleted by disappearing vegetation and contamination of the seas. Water supplies are being increasingly contaminated. The sky has become an open sewer. The conditions of life on this planet are running down.

The second and related cause of despair grows out of imperfect human organization. The ease with which human aggregations can organize for destructive purposes is exceeded only by their difficulty in meeting common survival problems. The human race is primed for apocalyptic war but not for enduring peace. The effect on the individual is to make life tentative, dispiriting.

The third cause of helplessness and hopelessness is onrushing depersonalization. The new technology has produced the theoretical basis for the greatest liberation from drudgery in human history, yet the pervasive effect has not been availability of new options but the quantification of life. Human beings in a world of computerized intelligence are taking on a quality of codified artifacts; they are losing their faces. They are also losing their secrets. Their mistakes and indiscretions are metabolized by a data base, never to be forgotten. Nothing is more universal than human fallibility; nothing is more essential than forgiveness or absolution. Yet statistical maintenance is as remorseless as it is free of redeeming judgments nourished by intangibles or the passing of time. Hope must be associated with names, not numbers. Helplessness, therefore, increases in direct proportion to numbering mechanisms that are unaffected by acts of faith or grand leaps of intuitive splendor.

The fourth cause of helplessness and hopelessness is related to a timeless condition: the dread of ultimate loneliness. It is here that existentialism has its greatest lure. The eternal quest of individual human beings is to shatter their loneliness. It is this condition that enables philosophers and theologians to make common cause with poets and artists. Loneliness is multidimensional. There is the loneliness of mortality. There is the loneliness of time that passes too slowly, or too swiftly. There is the loneliness of inevitable separation. There is the loneliness of alienation. There is the loneliness of aspiration. There is the loneliness of squandered dreams. There is the collective loneliness of the species, unable to proclaim its oneness in a world chained to its tribalisms.

And now, finally, there is the loneliness of life in the universe, always a philosophical preoccupation but now a presiding reality reinforced by man's forays into space. The change is greater than was represented by the Copernican revolution. Copernicus's contribution was primarily to knowledge, only secondarily to philosophy. After Copernicus, there was the challenge to the human mind that came from knowing that the earth was not the center of all things—but this challenge did not substantially change the fact that human beings continued to see themselves as the hub of the universe. People were astounded that previous generations ever believed that the earth did not revolve around the sun; but they continued to see themselves as being at the center of things.

But that was a long time ago. Humanity in the modern world has new outlooks, does it not?

In our time, the liberation of human beings from earth gravity has enabled the species to become less theoretical about, and less detached from, the universe. What was most significant about the lunar voyage was not that men set foot on the moon but that they set eye on the earth. They perceived larger relationships. They had an increased sense of human uniqueness. The effect was philosophical. To be able to rise from the earth; to be able, from a station in outer space, to see the relationship of the planet earth to other planets; to be able to contemplate the billions of factors in precise and beautiful combination that make human existence possible; to be able to meditate on journeying through an infinity of galaxies; to be able to dwell upon an encounter of the human brain and spirit with the universe—all this enlarges the human horizon. It also offers proof that technology is subordinate to human imagination; we went to the moon not because of our technology but because of our imagination. An objective had first to be conceived. The conception fathered the technology. The technology became successful only through the application not just of human intelligence but of willpower and aspiration as well.

Are you suggesting that we are putting our helplessness behind us?

Humans are not helpless. They have never been helpless. They have only been deflected or deceived or dispirited. This is not to say their history has not been pockmarked by failure. But failure is not the ultimate fact of life; it is an aspect of life in which transient or poor judgments play larger roles than they ought to. So long as people do not persuade themselves they are creatures of failure; so long as they have a vision of life as it ought to be; so long as they comprehend the full meaning and power of the unfettered mind—so long as this is so—they can look at the world and, beyond that, at the universe, with the sense that they can be unafraid of their fellow humans and can face choices not with dread but with great expectations.

I am not sure I see the connection between existentialism and the central purpose of our discussion, which is concerned with the quest for immortality and the relationship of human life to the universal order.

Since existentialism placed man in the center of the stage, it inevitably rejected the things or the ideas that have tried to organize man and control him. In this sense, existentialism has been described as "a reaction of the philosophy of man against the excesses of the philosophy of ideas and the philosophy of things." Thus, a certain relationship emerges between the possible moral implications of existentialism and some ideas of Friedrich von Schelling and Immanuel Kant. Indeed, defenders of existentialism have invoked Socrates' deathbed discourse as a sort of moral description of their own position. ("I do not know what lies in the beyond, but I go forward with courage and hope, and I shall find out in good time.") But Socrates was a philosophical activist and positivist.

He emphasized the need for hope and confidence; he was not depressed by the unknowable.

You make it sound as though man is minimized by existentialism.

The existentialist is detached from the larger body of which he is a part. He is preoccupied with the inevitability of personal death and recognizes no aspect of connection. He is therefore nonresponsible for the effects of his actions that may live after him.

The moment man becomes separated from his larger self, or the human totality, he tends to deny the moral content in the affairs of humans and of the universe itself. The concept of justice becomes inverted; i.e., he regards justice in largely subjective terms whereas justice, in order to become manifest, must have its own form and substance—which are absolute and eternal and which hold meaning. One of the principal gains in human development is represented by definitions of justice applied to specific situations. This is what is meant by codified law.

The individual is the ultimate cause, but that cause is defeated if individuals proclaim it for themselves. It is the difference between saying "I am as good as you are" and "You are as good as I am." The former statement leads to a breakdown of affirmative and social values. The latter statement prepares the ground for towers of purpose and achievement. Thus, some existential interpreters deny the identification and mutuality that make true justice possible.

But an even more basic weakness of existentialism is that it deals with life as random effect rather than as vital event. Indeed, the "meaninglessness of existence" is a phrase that often recurs in discussions of existentialism. For all practical purposes, life to the existentialist may actually be an illusion.

But long before existentialism, weren't important thinkers speculating on the possibility that life might be an illusion? Would you say that all those thinkers were negative or nihilist?

Certainly not. The notion of the universe as an illusion is a perfectly respectable philosophical idea and not necessarily negative. But when you put this idea in an existentialist setting, it takes on a somber coloration. It is precisely because life can be meaningful— even though you believe life may be an illusion—that we make this point.

What does your last sentence mean?

Significance can be attached to life independently of the argument over illusion versus reality. Philosophically speaking, the question of reality or illusion cannot be decided by objective proof, because the examining mechanism is the human mind, which is then trained on itself. Objective proof in this case would have to come from something outside the ken or scope of humankind. We may enlarge our objective techniques and even our knowledge, but we cannot change the basic fact that our position in contemplating the great questions is inherently subjective. But all these matters are besides the main point.

What is the main point?

Just that the question of universal illusion is irrelevant. The significance of life is not to be found in theories of illusion or reality, but in life itself. Humanity's lack of an objective position from which to contemplate ourselves need not cripple us philosophically or spiritually. Whatever the nature of the universe of which we are a part, we have minds and bodies that interact with other minds and bodies and with our full environment. That interaction has consequences, good and bad. And we most profitably can address ourselves to the fact of such consequences. What is truly meaningless is preoccupation with the "meaninglessness of existence." To repeat, we may not be able to prove objectively what we are or what we are part of, but such objective proof is of minor importance alongside the fact of interaction and consequence.

You mean to say that even though it could be demonstrated that life is actually an illusion, such a fact does not logically lead to the conclusion that existence is meaningless?

Precisely. For all we know, the universe, instead of being a vast something, might be a vast nothing, and we would still be justified in attaching meaning to life.

You speak of a "vast" nothingness. How can nothingness be "vast"? And how can life be meaningful if there is only "nothingness" in the universe?

It is quite possible to have a concept of nothingness in which something exists. For example, no vacuum is perfect. Shall we have a philosophical exercise by way of exploring the idea that there can be a "something" in "nothing" and that this "something" can be meaningful? Our first question has to do with the nature of the universe. What would you say the universe is?

Is there anything complicated about it? The universe is space, matter, and energy. Isn't that what the universe is?

What about the source of its power? What is reality on the universal scale? Is "the universe" synonymous with "infinity," or is it a product of "infinity," or what? In short, what do we really know about the universe?

Well, we know what we see, don't we? We know that our world is part of something infinitely vast, for we see all around us the evidence of a Great Design.

I am glad you said that, for it helps me to sharpen my question. This evidence that you observe about you has led you to make certain conclusions or assumptions about the universe, such as the fact that it consists of space, matter, energy, et cetera.

Yes.

And are you sure that those conclusions are right?

No, but you haven't told me what is wrong about them.

I merely intended to raise some questions. Isn't it possible that our own deficiencies, or limitations, in our own faculties of observation or methods of observation affect our idea of the universe? People were convinced by their faculties for many centuries that the earth had to be flat. Our sense of observation told us that if two people walked in opposite directions, starting from a given point, they would get farther away from each other.

But then to the faculty of surface observations was added analytical comprehension—in short, the scientific method—and people eventually realized that the earth was round. What seemed an apparent absurdity—namely, that people could meet each other if they got farther and farther apart—turned out to be scientifically accurate. In short, people began to think in much broader terms than the old yardsticks made possible. Those old yardsticks were only good for limited purposes, such as laying the foundations for a house, or measuring a strip of land. As soon as people had to address themselves seriously to larger concepts—such as their contemplation of the world or the universe—they began to discover the need for different and better yardsticks.

We are talking, of course, about what is known as a changing frame of reference. This involves, doesn't it, the interchangeability of absolutes and relatives?

Is it possible for them to be interchangeable?

Your absolutes and relatives change as your frame of reference changes. Let's take the universe, for example. Can you conceive of the universe existing if it was the size of an atom? I ask this question as part of the exercise I referred to a moment ago. This exercise is designed to show that life can be meaningful even if there is no objective proof of reality.

The entire universe the size of an atom? No, I cannot conceive of a universe that small, if you mean that it would still have inside it all the things that go to make up a universe as I understand it.

Very well, then. Let us proceed step by step. Suppose you were half your size, and everything about you was half its size— myself, this room, the city, the state, the nation, the world, and the universe itself. Would you be aware of the difference?

Well, if everything was reduced proportionately, I don't think I could tell the difference.

We have now succeeded in reducing the universe to half its present size. The parts of that universe maintain fixed relativity— that is, they still bear the same relationship to each other inside an absolute whole.

Yes, but where is this leading us?

We've still got a long way to shrink before we get where we're going. Having reduced the universe in half, we now reduce it in half again . . . and again . . . and again. But each time we maintain the exact proportions. And since you have no sense of absolute size, for your measuring rods are also reduced proportionately, you have no way of knowing you are now one-sixteenth of your former size—or do you?

No, I don't see how I could know that, or prove it even if I did suspect it. Is that what you meant when you said that things are absolute only within a fixed frame of reference?

Yes. They are absolute in the sense that they maintain their same relative positions. Let us continue with our theoretical shrinkage. You are now one-sixteenth of your former size. I ask you to conceive of this process going on almost indefinitely. Can you conceive of yourself, for example, as being no larger than what you now recognize as a microscopic particle? Everything else, of course, would be in the same proportion.

Yes, but it is getting difficult.

It needn't be, since the proportions remain the same. Now keep shrinking your frame of reference until you are on an atomic scale.

I'll try.

Now reduce yourself further still within the atom so that everything you can conceive of in the observable world and the world beyond that—indeed, your conception of the universe itself—everything is contained within a space no larger than an atomic particle.

And the proportions still remain the same inside the particle?

Yes.

Then, I guess I couldn't tell the difference.

Having done that, I ask you now to take the biggest, or rather, the smallest, hurdle of all. Do you know what a meson is?

I believe it is one of the smallest of the subatomic particles.

Precisely. It is one of the smallest particles known to scientists. For all intents and purposes, it is without size. But its effects can be felt. It is not nearly so small as the neutrino, which is theoretically the smallest thing we know of, but it is much more interesting because its energy has a finite lifetime.

I want to ask you to imagine that everything in the universe has been compressed into such a space. In this sense, through relativity, we try to put everything inside nothing.

You deflated my ego earlier when you spoke of immortality. Now there is nothing left of it at all.

On the contrary, your ego wouldn't even know it had been shrunk so long as it was still large enough to assert itself in relation to other things.

But I still don't see what significance you attach to the fact that it is possible for everything to be inside something the size of a meson or what part this could have in my philosophy.

I will come to that. Right now I have done only half my job. You conceded that you could exist even though you may be smaller than what might be considered to be practically nothing. Having disposed of matter and space, we address ourselves to time. Let us go through the same process as before. Let us suppose that all the clocks in the world would move twice as fast, that the planets would revolve at twice their speed, that your senses were twice as fast, that everything grew or decayed at the same increase in speed. So long as this increase was constant in every respect, would you be able to tell the difference?

You mean I would live only half as long, but since everything is twice as fast, it would be as though I had lived my full life? Well, in that case, I don't suppose I would know the difference.

Very well, let us continue to speed up this time factor until finally your entire life takes place within what we now regard as a minute. So long as your capacity to live, think, and act is similarly speeded up, you would have no way of discerning any difference.

Now comes the final step. One of the shortest time sequences known to science is the half-life of the same meson we referred to earlier. This half-life of the meson is a microsecond cut into more than a million parts. Let us take one of these parts and theoretically subdivide it further so that it encompasses not only your entire life, not only all the ages of man, but the age of the universe itself. Galileo was fond of speculating upon the subdivisions of time until they became what he called "infinite instants." Do you agree that so long as the subdivisions remain constant in our meson, relativistically speaking, things would be as they are now, at least to your apparent senses?

Yes, I guess so.

What we have just done, of course, is to take everything inside our existing frame of reference and shift it to a theoretically smaller frame of reference by making such proportionate reductions as may be required to fit. You might argue, of course, that while a meson in the big frame of reference occupies a fixed size, it would be proportionately reduced and still remain a meson in the smaller frame of reference.

I like logic, but I am not sure I follow this. A moment ago I thought I could follow this line of reasoning. Now you have lost me completely.

What I just said was intended to meet the argument that as man is reduced in size, the meson is reduced with him. According to this argument, therefore, no matter how small a man gets, he cannot become as small as the meson, because the meson becomes proportionately smaller at the same time. It might also be argued that the functions of certain units in the universe are absolutely dependent upon an absolute size. But our exercise was predicated on the fact that the meson would be constant while our shrinking process was going on. The meson was theoretically the same while we kept cutting the universe in half and kept doubling the time factor until the universe became smaller than the fixed, or hypothetically absolute, size of the meson.

Now I see what you meant when you referred earlier to the interchangeability of absolutes and relatives.

Actually, I was trying to do something more important than to demonstrate that the absolute and the relative are not inconsistent and indeed are twin aspects of the universal order. The main purpose of our reduction sequence was to suggest that even if our universe is nothing more than an atomic speck, it is large enough to have vital significance through the interaction of one life with another and, in a larger sense, the interaction of all time, space, matter, and energy. We may never be able to prove in absolute terms that life is not an illusion, but it is within our capacity to comprehend that there is a consequential reality, and that this reality depends less on dimension than on interrelationship and effect.

May I ask, how do we know that the universe really isn't as small as you have hypothetically made it?

It may well be. In a sense, the universe may be conceived of as the smallest total unit of infinity.

You keep talking about the universe and infinity as though they were different things. Doesn't the universe embrace infinity?

It all depends on how we use the terms. I make a distinction in order to separate two related, though different, concepts. The universe, its system, order, energy, matter, space, time—all of these are different aspects or manifestations of the same "thing." The "thing" itself may be absolute, but its aspects are relativistic. Infinity transcends both absolutes and relatives. How would you define infinity?

I once heard a definition of infinity that appealed to me. It was that infinity was larger than the largest thing I could think of.

Would it follow from your definition that the largest thing or unit you could think of could be regarded as the smallest thing or unit in infinity?

It might.

Paraphrasing this, might it not also be said that the universe has something of a frame of reference—while infinity does not? In the existing universal frame of reference, the frame itself may or may not be absolute, but at least the components are relative. Infinity is independent of size. It is neither large nor small, according to our limited notions of absolute and relative size. Attempts to view it in terms of dimension are as meaningless as the attempt to find the earth precipice to hell in the Middle Ages. Infinity eludes human imagination. It may not even be a function. It is that which lies beyond size and concept and, possibly, function. It is neither relative nor absolute. In fact, it is what the universe is not. It is a field for the relativistic unit that comprises the universal essence— that essence being the interaction and interchangeability of space, time, energy, matter. Now, what did you say your idea of infinity was, again?

I said it was larger than the largest thing I could think of.

Would you now be willing to modify that definition to say that it is a field, of which the universe as we conceive it may be only a speck?

I think so. In other words, I may actually be as small as your reduction sequence pictured me?

Perhaps even smaller, but size is not important. Function and essence are what count. Our tiny universe may be lost in infinity, but it operates and has an essence. And even within the universe itself, the separate parts or aspects may seem so minute as to be nonexistent within the whole, but each of these parts has its own significance. Each of these parts is none the less functional for being part of the universal void.

Did you say "void"?

Yes. I might more accurately have said "vacuum." How would you define a vacuum?

A vacuum is nothing; no, I mean a vacuum is something that contains nothing. But that doesn't sound right—something containing nothing . . .

On the contrary, it is an excellent description. We have vacuums in our laboratories—things that try to contain nothing. I say "try" because, for all our inventiveness, we have never succeeded in producing a perfect vacuum. We have never been able to create a perfect nothingness. In spite of our most ingenious efforts, something remains in the vacuum. There are always a few molecules left floating around. And yet we feel justified in calling it a vacuum because it serves the purposes of a vacuum. Now, can you imagine the same thing as being true of the universe?

You mean, can I imagine the universe as a vacuum?

Yes.

Frankly, I cannot. There are too many stars and planets and Milky Ways and galaxies for me to do that. All I have to do is to walk outside on a cool night and look up at the star-studded sky. My answer would be, literally, heavens no.

But you can accept the idea of a vacuum in which molecules exist?

Certainly.

All those stars and planets you are talking about are actually the molecules of universal space. And there are fewer of them, and they are relatively smaller in number, than the molecules in the finest vacuum produced in our laboratories.

You mean that the matter in space is actually so rare as to make the universe a vacuum?

Yes, for all intents and purposes. It is a vacuum so nearly perfect that, try as we might in our laboratories, we have never succeeded in approaching anything like it, with respect to the ratio of total matter to total space. And yet, what is important here is not the dominant nature of universal space, but the fact that molecules or stars and solar systems *do* exist.

Can we go back a bit? I was just wondering why scientists have never been able to create a perfect vacuum. Are there any theories about this?

All we know is that the creation of a perfect vacuum may be more difficult than the splitting of an atom. We have been unable to eliminate all the molecules floating around after we have expelled matter from the vacuum. It may be that the answer to the ultimate universal force lies in the mystery of the imperfect vacuum—whether in our laboratories or in the universe. Perhaps it is the phenomenon of the vacuum that we ought to be scrutinizing for the approach to our ultimate answers rather than the mystery of infinity. The universal force may be manifest in the natural resistance to absolute nothingness. Putting it another way, we ought to be directing our energies and speculations to the significance of the simple fact that absolute nothingness is impossible.

I don't see anything so simple about that.

It is simple only in the sense that we don't have to send spaceships out into the Solar System to search for the nature of the universal force. The exploration and contemplation of a void might offer richer meaning for our quest of the nature of ultimate force.

You have made the statement that nothingness is impossible. Can you expand on that?

It is impossible either to conceive of absolute nothingness or to create absolute nothingness. Isn't it possible that the reason we say that something is created out of nothing is because our senses are conscious of the something but cannot conceive of the nothing? May it not be that there has never been an absolute nothingness? Whatever the force is that keeps nothingness from becoming absolute may be what we have in mind when we talk about creation.

Are you saying that whatever it is that keeps a somethingness from becoming a nothingness—in the vacuum or the universal void—is where ultimate force begins?

Let's modify that. Not where it begins, but where it exists. Since nothingness is not only the total absence of matter but also the total absence of time, this ultimate force must therefore be independent of time and matter; but the "something" that it creates can have both. Thus, the point at which the vacuum is about to become complete, but does not, may be the point at which universal reality manifests itself.

I am not sure I follow this. Do you mean that something happens in the universal vacuum whenever it seems to drop below certain critical limits with respect to universal matter or energy?

That's a good way of putting it. It doesn't make much difference whether we regard this as a process of resistance or conversion; there are critical limits below which the level of universal substance does not fall. In fact, our scientists say that new cosmic matter is being created all the time. We live in an expanding universe. As I suggested, the sum total of all our solar systems and galaxies may be as nothing in the total scheme, but they are everything in the more limited scheme in which they function. And they have essence.

Function and essence are everything, then?

Function and essence count for a great deal, but they may not be everything. Indeed, so far as human beings are concerned, the uniqueness of humanity lies in a something that is beyond function and essence. Just as infinity may be defined as that which lies inside and also beyond universal space, so the uniqueness of man may be defined as the "something" that lies beyond function and essence.

I don't know what "something" means when you say there is a "something" that lies beyond function and essence. What "something"?

That is what has engrossed the theologians and philosophers ever since humanity began to think about itself. There has never been a more fascinating subject to command the human imagination. The "something" that lies beyond function and essence in man and that constitutes his uniqueness cannot adequately be described by any single term. Even "the individual's spirit" and "capacity for faith"—however poetic and evocative—are not the sum total of human uniqueness. "Perception" and "awareness" and "conscience" represent other elements of his uniqueness without exhausting them. "Love," "compassion," and "sense of kinship" are characteristics within the capacity of man, but they, too, are part of a larger whole. Similarly, "intelligence," "imagination," "command of historical experience," and "ability to inspire and be inspired" are other parts of this whole but not the whole itself.

Just as it is necessary to think of infinity as lacking a specific form or even a specific substance, so humankind's uniqueness defies mere verbalization and exists in its combined manifestations. One might also say that this uniqueness is manifest in existence itself.

4

Inevitability
As a
Universal Law

We have been discussing infinity at length. Now we should consider an aspect of infinity that apparently defies logic. It is that infinity converts what is possible into the inevitable.

The statement, as you have said, defies logic. It is incomprehensible without an example.

Perhaps the best way of illuminating the statement is to refer to the possibility of life on other planets. Along with immortality, the question of sentient life in the universe has always engaged the inquisitive mind. But this question is no longer abstract or fanciful. It has become a matter of considerable pertinence. Yet one's concept of infinity is critical in such speculations. A limited notion of infinity inhibits the concept that life—life with intelligence and sensitivity and the capacity for perfectibility—exists elsewhere in the universe.

Why must an uncircumscribed definition of infinity lead to the conclusion that life exists on other planets?

If the frame of reference is not large enough, it cannot contain all the possibilities. The Solar System is not unique in the universe. It is unscientific to say that among the many billions of other celestial systems, there are no other planets that support life in advanced form. Nature shuns one of a kind as much as it abhors a vacuum. If this idea is difficult to accept, just increase your idea of the universe by as many billions of planets as may be required to accommodate a reasonable basis for believing that highly differentiated life-forms exist—or even abound—in the universe.

I can enlarge my concept of infinity, but I still don't see why that ought to lead to the conclusion that what is possible becomes inevitable in infinity.

Infinity applies to both space and time. Therefore, the principle of exclusivity does not exist in the universe. If anything occurs at one place or at one time in the universe, it is bound to occur at another, given infinite time and infinite space. Another way of saying this is that the possible becomes the inevitable whenever there are no limits on laws of chance.

I can follow the reasoning that the probability of occurrence increases in direct ratio to the widening of chance, but I am not sure I see that, because solar systems similar to ours abound in the universe, life is certain to exist.

The same conditions that make life possible make life inevitable. Yet our collective ego blurs our view, and we don't ask the primary question. The primary question ought to be: How did the conditions that make life possible originate? How did they come together in vital confluence? The interaction of these precise and exquisite conditions forces life into being. So long as these conditions continue to interact, life is inevitable. Infinity supplies the stage.

Life in human form?

The life process. Once the life process begins, the development into highly differentiated forms is as natural as the process itself. There is no shortage of theories—the Darwinian theory being one of them—to explain the gradual, and at times mutant, differentiation of life into human form.

You are saying, then, that once the conditions exist that are congenial to the life process, life becomes inevitable.

Correct.

But what if some terrible catastrophe would occur that would destroy life without also destroying the conditions that make life possible? Assume, hypothetically, that a nuclear war breaks out on earth and that the radioactive firestorms sweeping over the earth destroy the human population. Would human life start up all over again?

If the conditions are destroyed that make human life possible, human life would not start up again. But if a manmade catastrophe did not destroy the basic conditions of life, then the life process would assert itself. What forms life would then take would depend on the nature of the conditions prevailing. Conceivably, a blanket of radioactivity might produce substantially new life-forms by radically changing, rather than totally eliminating, the conditions of life. Our essential point, therefore, is that life is the product of its conditions. This would hold on other planets throughout the universe as well.

So that it is in the nature of infinity that anything that is possible is certain to happen? How can I verify this hypothesis with my own senses?

If you can wait long enough and look in enough places, you can look to your senses for verification. Otherwise, you have to look to your power of reasoning. The fact of infinity, large though it is, is still approachable by the human mind. In fact, now that we have entered the stage of space exploration, it is by no means inconceivable that human observation, rather than theory alone, will be able to confirm the prevalence of life in the universe.

I suppose I ought to find all these new developments exhilarating, but I confess I'm not sure I welcome them. It's difficult enough getting used to the fact that our species may not be of primary importance in the universe without having to contemplate the possibility that life in advanced form may exist on numberless planets. I feel minimized by these ideas.

The process of growing up as a species is not too different from the process of growing up as an individual. We come of age as a cosmic species when we accept the fact that the universe does not exist for our exclusive convenience. The first big jolt to the species-ego came, as we said earlier, when Copernicus discovered that the earth is not the center of all things. Even after the human species adjusted to the Copernican reality, it persisted in believing that the universe was designed with human life at the center. Now we must make our peace with the reality that, though we may be a highly privileged species, we may not be one of a kind. We must adjust, finally, to the fact that the universe may not be constructed for our particular benefit.

I doubt that I can grow up that fast. My entire conditioning, spiritual and philosophical, has been keyed to the uniqueness of human life in the universe. It is unreasonable to expect me not to feel diminished.

Far from feeling diminished, we ought to feel a sense of privilege. A great adventure opens out before us. We have new worlds to contemplate. We have new connections to make. A rendezvous with infinity becomes us.

In a relative sense, life is still rare enough to suit the most demanding species-ego. But what is important about life is not that it may or may not be unique. What is most important is that whatever its place in infinity, life is infinitely precious. It is precious because of what it is, not because of any universal prevalence it may have.

It is precious because the human mind can contemplate questions such as these. We do not have to experience infinity in order to encompass it.

It is precious because we have access to the phenomenon of cause and effect, thus being able to create our own causes and to shape our own effects. We can dwell on the experiences of past lives and thus enhance our own time.

One of the main purposes of education is to identify causes and to anticipate effects. Civilization advances in direct proportion to our ability to not repeat past errors. We will never become error free; the circumstances of life change and provide abundant opportunities for new mistakes. But past mistakes, properly perceived, can help us deal with new ones and also control or reduce their consequences.

Life is precious not because it is perfectible but because human beings can comprehend the idea of perfectibility. It is precious because there are no limits to the fineness of human sensitivities. We are capable of responding to the good, the true, and the beautiful. We have the capacity to love and to respond to love.

Life is precious because of the faculty of creativity. We can use the senses to enliven and nourish the senses. We can create forms and sounds and images that give meaning and splendor to life. We can do things for the first time. We can create in ways we have never created before. We can do the impossible.

Finally, nothing about human life is more precious than that we can define our own purpose and shape our own destiny.

All my intellectual training has pointed me in the direction of looking for human purpose outside myself and for searching for an objective concept of human destiny. Are you saying that all this lies within ourselves—that we are able to fashion our basic purpose and to shape our destiny? Aren't you impinging on divine prerogatives?

It adds to, and does not detract from, a concept of the Deity to say that humankind is divinely endowed to perceive its own purpose and to create its own destiny.

I may be able to define a purpose that suits me. Other persons may have different definitions. This adds up to bedlam and perhaps worse.

True enough. I wasn't thinking of aggregations of human beings attempting to impose their views of human purpose or human destiny on one another. I was thinking of your capacity—the capacity of the individual—to find within yourself what you regard as essential human purpose. This does not mean that your search for truth need be confined. You can respond to truth as perceived by others. It is your own recognition, from whatever source, of the nature of human purpose and human destiny that is vital.

Do you have a definition of human purpose you would have me consider?

I would have you consider that the highest purpose of the human species is to justify the gift of life.

We do this in many ways: by being aware of its preciousness and its fragility; by developing to the fullest the potentialities and sensitivities that come with life; by putting the whole of our intelligence to work in sustaining and enhancing the conditions that make life possible; by cherishing the human habitat and shielding it from devastation and depletion; by using our free will to the utmost in advancing the cause of life; finally, by celebrating life.

But human beings have different values. Not all of them cherish life. What reason is there to believe they can do or will want to do these things?

The question is not whether human beings are prepared to do these things. The question is whether you, the individual, are prepared to do it. You have the gift of free will. You can make choices. So long as the ability to choose can be matched with options of consequence, there are strong grounds for hope. There is hope that enough individuals will use their free will to make the life-giving and life-sustaining choices.

What are the choices that test the free will of the individual?

Each individual is capable of both great altruism and great venality. He has it within his means to extend the former and exorcise the latter.

The individual is capable of both great compassion and great indifference. He has it within his means to nourish the former and outgrow the latter.

The individual is capable of maintaining great societies and staging great holocausts. He has it within his means to fortify the former and avert the latter.

The individual is capable of ennobling life and disfiguring it. He has it within his means to assert the former and anathematize the latter.

If he recognizes that his basic purpose is to justify his humanity, he will have no difficulty in addressing himself to these choices.

Basic purpose and human destiny do not lie outside him, but within him.

I would like to think that human destiny can be what we want it to be, but I wonder whether we may not have been put here for a purpose over which we have no control. Is it not conceivable that we have a place in the universal design that we will never be in a position to alter, however strong our free will and however majestic our acceptance of the need to justify our humanity?

Humanity's next great development may be our liberation from the idea that we have no command over our destiny. Even if it could be demonstrated that we are moving steadily toward a negative destiny, we may be able to change direction.

I have trouble comprehending such a hypothesis.

Let me give an example by way of supporting the statement that human beings could change their "apparent" destiny. Let us assume we discover that our purpose on earth is to play a part in making this planet into a nova through a hydrogen-helium reaction. The theory is not altogether fanciful. Throughout the universe, planets become stars with great frequency. This may be one of the ways the universe receives a new infusion of energy. A nova, or star, is a ball of fire, like the sun. The "fire" is actually a hydrogen-helium reaction. Science has only the vaguest theories as to the cause of the phenomenon—that is, what causes a planet to become a star.

Suppose we discover that sentient creatures helped to bring about this result. Let us further hypothesize that such sentient life had some of the characteristics associated with the human species—the capacity for progress or the ability to invent and create. Suppose we learned that the species' inventive intelligence interacted, as it does in humans on earth, with its basic instability and belligerence. It is not illogical to imagine that the spiraling consequence was a series of acts of massive and convulsive violence. Nor is it illogical to suppose that increasingly devastating means were employed, culminating in the use of fission and fusion explosives. At the point of massive fusion detonations, a hydrogen-helium reaction was set off involving the entire planetary mass. So the planet became a star, and the universe had a new infusion of energy.

Suppose it could be demonstrated, as I say, that this cosmic eventuality is the underlying purpose of human life on earth. How would you react?

I would be appalled. I don't see how I could be expected to believe it.

This is precisely my point. Considerations of human destiny tend to be confined within a narrow range of possibilities, all of them auspicious. Why must the basic purpose of human life be confined to that which is satisfying to the human ego? If we come to believe that the universe receives constant new infusions of energy through new hydrogen-helium reactions, then we might be serving a higher purpose in triggering the conversion process.

You don't seriously believe that the purpose of intelligent life is to follow a predetermined path of evolution and invention leading to the conversion of the earth into a ball of fire?

I am not advocating the theory. What I am attempting to do is to get you to examine its implications as a theoretical possibility. Assume, therefore, that human beings may be the missing link in the process by which a planet becomes a star.

Such a destiny may not be beyond my comprehension, but it is beyond my spiritual digestive capacity. When I contemplate the totality of human existence—the long trail of human evolution, all the aspiration and suffering and achievement, all the science and poetry and art—I find it inconceivable that all this could end in a cosmic bang. What a terrible joke on all our theology and philosophy! No, I recoil from the hypothesis. I have to continue to think of human beings as creatures with a destiny compatible with their intelligence and nobility, not as cosmic dynamiters and igniters of universal fuses.

If you can't accept such a destiny, can you accept the reality that you have the capacity and the obligation to change it?

But human destiny, almost by definition, is something that can't be changed.

Then change the definition. This is precisely my point. Nothing is more representative of human uniqueness than the ability of humans to define and pursue their own destiny. My hypothetical exercise about a planet's becoming a nova was designed to suggest that even if it could be proved that our destiny is to supply the universe with new energy, we are not without affirmative options.

You mean we could deflect ourselves from such a terrifying purpose? What options do we have?

If the human race actually came to believe that its purpose was to convert a planet into a star, it could direct its inventiveness into ways of accomplishing that purpose without converting our planet into a ball of fire.

How could we convert our planet into a star without its becoming a ball of fire?

It wouldn't have to be our own planet. We can use our knowledge and our capacity for ranging far out into the universe in order to accomplish the same purpose. If in fact there are universal requirements for new energy, and if we recognize that our purpose is connected to these requirements, then we have the means for creating hydrogen-helium reactions on lifeless planets or spatial masses. We can do so through careful planning as an act of intelligence and free will.

Are you suggesting that we ought to embark on an immediate program for sending spaceships out into the universe to blow up selected planets?

Certainly not. I have offered a theoretical example designed to show that even under circumstances where it would appear that we were moving toward a destiny that did not enhance our view of life, we would not be without recourse. We have the ability to transcend all apparent or theoretical or actual limitations. Our purpose in the universe is in our own hands. This is what makes us unique.

So we venture out into space, lighting candles here and there, in the universe? Doesn't this require us to be godlike?

This, too, is within our means. The ability to create choices and to choose correctly may be the ultimate divine gift. Being able to make the fulfilling choice may be the highest exercise of our intelligence and spirituality. Once again, to paraphrase Descartes, we are human; therefore, we justify life.

5

The Human Brain
As
Cosmos

Earlier, we spoke about human life as the rarest prize in the universe. Perhaps the best way to convey some sense of the spectacular nature of the prize is to ask you to estimate the number of planets in the universe.

I wouldn't even know how to begin to guess.

Even the astronomers, with all their advanced instrumentation, can only come up with guesses. The principal fact turned up by astronomical technology is that there are galaxies beyond the range of our instruments. Whether there are two billion or ten billion or twenty billion planets is not relevant here. It is enough for our purposes that we can congratulate ourselves that the planet earth exists and has all the delicate balances that make human life possible. To begin with, therefore, we are dealing with the ultimate prize that the universe has to offer—a planet that can support and sustain life. But this is only the beginning.

How much more of a prize can there be?

Let's look at life on this planet. How many different forms of life are there on the planet?

I suppose the scientists could come up with a more precise answer than they do about the number of planets. But I find myself in the same position of not even being able to guess.

If we are talking about all animate forms on earth, the number would probably be in excess of several billion. And of all those forms, the only one that possesses the attributes of advanced intelligence is the human species. In belonging to that species, you are the beneficiary of a triumph over incredible odds. But that is not all.

You mean that there are other odds to describe the rarity of human life?

I have in mind the particular rarity that is you. Apart from your presence in the universe, several million other "selves" competed with you for the privilege of being born. You were one of millions of sperm cells struggling for union with the female egg cell. Each one of those sperm cells contained all the ingredients and characteristics that go to make up a separate and complete human being.

We might have an enlarged appreciation of our individual selves if we realized how much of a victory over indescribably long odds our appearance as human beings represents. We take this victory for granted—just as we take for granted other things of infinite mystery. When we look at another species—a horse, a dog, a cat—do we have an appropriate sense of wonder about a form of life so different from our own that it might very well have originated on another planet?

I confess that when I look at a horse or a dog or a cat, I have only affectionate feelings. I like to make friends with animals. Life would be a lot more barren than it is, if there were no animals.

But try to imagine that you had never heard of such animals and that you were looking at one of them for the first time. I suspect that your reaction would be no less stark than if you were actually in the presence of a creature from outer space.

Yes, I can imagine having such a sensation, but I am not sure why that is significant.

It is significant because no one has been able adequately to explain—philosophically, at least—the reason for different species, from a mite to a man. Our own species enjoys extraordinary endowments—a highly differentiated brain that makes it possible to create great collective societies that we call civilization; the ability to use language, not just for the purpose of expressing personal needs, but to convey abstract ideas. We can create art and literature. We can contemplate a past and anticipate a future. We also possess certain physical advantages—an opposing thumb, for example, that enables us to use complicated tools invented by our intelligence. Now, have you ever wondered why you enjoy these special attributes or gifts in contrast to most of the other species?

Actually, I have not particularly thought of myself as more fortunate than other animals.

But you do recognize a wide disparity between other forces of life and your own.

Yes, I am aware of the differences, but I'm not altogether certain we have used these differences to advantage.

Understandable, but doesn't the very fact of another species lay any claims on your imagination? A great gap between humans and other species gives rise to profound philosophical questions.

Didn't Darwin explain all this?

Darwin made no pretense of having answers to all the questions his theory raised. If the interacting factors of time, environmental conditions, and challenges to existence combine to produce major genetic or evolutionary change, why haven't we been able to observe such changes over the centuries? Room for speculative wonder still exists over the differences between the species—so much so that other animals provide an opportunity for us to become exquisitely aware of our own endowments, beginning with the human brain.

Earlier, you indicated that we lack a special station for the objective scrutiny of self. How can we become fully aware of the special qualities of the human brain if we have only our brain to scrutinize our brain?

The brain scrutinizing itself is probably the ultimate wonder— the use of intelligence to understand the source and workings of intelligence. What makes the exercise so formidable is that the human brain is a mirror to infinity.

Not even the universe, with its countless billions of galaxies, exceeds the human brain in wonder and complexity. There is no limit to its range, scope, or capacity for creative growth. It makes possible new perceptions and new perspectives, just as it clears the way for brighter prospects in human affairs.

If the brain of an average fifty-year-old person could be fully emptied of all the impressions and memories it has stored and recorded, the tape would reach to the moon and back several times. Indeed, it is possible that the memory contents of the human brain could never be fully inventoried; new impressions would come in faster than the old ones could be identified. Much has been said about the memory capability of the human brain. Silicon chips and semiconductors have been hailed as supreme achievements of technology. But these chips are far inferior to the neurons of the human brain in terms of function and mystery.

What do we know about the way the brain is constructed?

The average brain weighs approximately three pounds, accounting for about 2 percent of the body's total weight, yet consuming more than 20 percent of its oxygen.

The brain does most of its work through neurons—agents too small to be weighed or measured. No one knows how many neurons reside in the brain. The estimates move sharply upward decade after decade. As recently as 1950, brain researchers thought they were being extravagant when they guessed there might be as many as a billion neurons. Today, some estimates range from 50 to 100 billion. These neurons carry the traffic for millions of signals. The brain of someone reaching for just the precise word can set off millions of electrochemical reactions. When we visualize the face of someone we know, the same process occurs. In short, numberless signals are flashing almost every second of our waking hours. Hooking up our thoughts in sequence involves vast neural activity.

The main control console of the brain is the hypothalamus, a vital link between body and brain. Its situation below the cerebral cortex and atop the spine seems most appropriate for this purpose. This is where the basic drives of the body—sex, hunger, awareness of danger, and so forth—are located. Similar control is exercised by the hypothalamus over the pituitary gland, which governs the production and circulation of hormones for the body.

Nerves all over the body can be involved in transmitting information to the brain—information from the five senses and the organs, information about body movement, information of an emotional nature. Now it has become evident that many other substances circulating in the blood, besides hormones, make direct contact with brain centers as well.

All this sensory input, which begins in the brain, has its effects throughout the body. Few aspects of the brain are more fascinating or significant than the way it makes its registrations on the immune system. In this way, our thoughts can have an effect on health and our ability to turn back disease. Brain cells and immune cells are equipped for direct communication with one another.

The brain seems to be the only part of the body that is totally essential for individual identity. If we have a defective kidney or liver, or even heart, we can acquire a transplant and still retain our sense of self—who we are, what we have done or want to do, a knowledge of our commitments and our aspirations. But if we were to acquire a new brain—assuming that medical science could solve

the incredibly complex problems involved in a brain transplant—
we would also acquire a new self.

*It seems strange that the brain is able to discern so many things
about itself.*

The human brain is connected not just to the body, but to
the world and the universe around it. The forces involved in the
life of the planets—what keeps them in orbit, what they consist
of, what energizes them—are basic to human life. The same elec-
tromagnetic forces that govern the movements of the planets also
exist in the human body. Human blood in many respects is like a
great electrical river, carrying with it billions of charged particles
for maintaining and nourishing life. No construction or recon-
struction project is as complex or wide-ranging as the way the
human body repairs and sustains itself. Knowledge of this complexity, though vastly larger than it used to be, is grossly incomplete.
So much so, in fact, that the pursuit of new knowledge about the
inner universe of human beings may be the greatest frontier in
history.

*Are you saying that we know less about what goes on in human
beings than what goes on in the universe?*

It would be possible to make a very good argument for just
that proposition. Consider something as basic as the way the human
body heals itself. A great deal of knowledge has been accumulated
about the circulatory system, the nervous system, the endocrine
system, the digestive system, the autonomic nervous system, the
parasympathetic nervous system, and other systems. But no such

comparable knowledge has been developed about the healing system. If you read the index in a medical textbook, you will find separate listings for all the systems except the healing system. If you look in the *Merck Manual,* a one-volume reference book used in many medical schools, you will draw the same blank. If you turn to *Dorland's Illustrated Medical Dictionary,* you will find nothing under "healing system."

Isn't it possible that the reason is that healing involves all the body's systems?

Yes, all the body's systems are interconnected, yet each one has been studied separately and is fully charted. Not so the healing system—at least not until now.

Not until now?

Medical researchers are now exploring the vast terrain of healing, beginning with the way the human body protects itself against disease, and extending through the way the body seeks to turn back disease when it occurs. They are discovering connections between the belief system and the healing system. They are discovering the way all the body's systems are interconnected. They are discovering the way these systems communicate with one another, conveying needs and working together to meet them. They are discovering a far wider role for the human brain in maintaining health and in combating disease than had been realized.

The brain as an instrument of healing? I had thought that the brain was the seat of intelligence and the center of consciousness.

It is all that and more. The brain is a gland—for all we know, the most prolific gland in the human body. It has been known for a long time that the brain played a role in activating the body's hormones, but not until recently was it known just how large a role this is. Nor was it known how wide was the variety of hormones produced by the brain itself. Some of these hormones are the body's own painkillers. They contain morphinelike molecules. They are called endorphins or encephalins. "Endorphin" is a coined word: the first four letters refer to the fact that the process takes place inside the body; the last part of the word comes from "morphine." Similarly, "encephalin" is a coined word, the first part of which refers to the head; the second part of which also comes from "morphine."

These secretions, however, do more than help the body with pain. They are believed to have a triggering role in activating other hormones and substances vital to optimal human functioning. Sometimes we experience a flush of well-being, as, for example, after a good outing on the ski slopes or the tennis court or the jogging track. What happens is that the endorphins trigger the release of other hormones to create a feeling of well-being. But there are other equally wondrous hormones produced by the brain or activated by the brain.

What other hormones?

Some three dozen such hormones have been identified. Interferons, for example.

Does the word "interferon" have any connection with the word "interfere"?

You might regard it as such. At first it was thought that interferons "interfered" with the process of infections. Then it was found that interferon did all that and more.

More?

Yes. They discovered that interferons could fight viruses. Then came the most important finding of all. Interferons have a role in fighting cancer cells.

The brain also produces or activates gamma globulin, the substance that fortifies the body's immunological functions. What is most interesting of all about the brain as a gland is that it can combine these various secretions. Theoretically, therefore, the brain is capable of producing thousands of secretions to meet the body's varying needs.

Does the power of the brain have any relevance in fighting new diseases? Has it had any effect on AIDS, for example?

Studies of long-term AIDS survivors indicate several things. The first thing is that active defiance is a factor in contributing to longevity. Dr. Walter Cannon, in the 1930s, showed that heightened emotion, such as a blazing determination, could actually stimulate the spleen and produce an increase in the population of red blood cells. Later researchers discovered that the same process is involved with immune cells. This means that even though the T4 cells are destroyed by the AIDS virus—exposing the individual to increased susceptibility to serious disease—other components of the immune system may be capable of taking up part of the slack, at least. Some AIDS patients have lived ten years or more beyond the original diagnosis. A second factor in the extended longevity of these patients is that they felt that they were needed to help newly diagnosed patients deal with the emotional devastation caused by the diagnosis itself. Emotions have effects on the body's hormones. The brain can produce or activate the production of these hormones.

This makes it sound as though the human brain is a well-stocked apothecary.

Not the least impressive aspect of the brain's capability is the special connection of the brain not just to the body's endocrine system, but to the immune system. The interaction of these three systems has created the basis for an exciting new field of medicine named psychoneuroimmunology. This somewhat cumbersome new term describes the way the brain can interact with the endocrine system and the immune system.

Are you saying that there are actually changes in the way the body functions as the result of what goes on in the mind?

Probably the most important new area of knowledge in human health concerns the potentiating power of the human mind. If we are looking for a supreme manifestation of human uniqueness, it may well be in the way the mind is able to raise human capacity to meet difficult challenges.

Are you just speaking poetically, or are you referring to something that has been scientifically established?

I am referring to scientific findings. These findings began with the biological effects of negative emotions.

Negative emotions cover a very wide field. I can think of hate, fear, panic, rage, exasperation, frustration, depression, anxiety. Am I to believe that these negative feelings can actually have biological effects?

Sometimes seriously so. For example, there are studies to show that prolonged grief can cause serious illness. Medical researchers have been able to show a connection between bereavement and cancer. Two thousand years ago, one of the major figures in medicine, Galen, perceived a connection between melancholy and malignancy. That observation has been confirmed many times since. Modern medical literature contains hundreds of references to studies linking depression, anguish, anxiety, despair, or other forms of severe emotional stress to the onset of many diseases.

You refer only to the adverse or negative emotions. Don't the positive emotions have their effects? If depression or despair or anxiety can help bring on disease, why couldn't hope or love or faith or confidence or a strong will to live or deep purpose help to combat disease?

You have correctly raised what is one of the most important questions in medicine being researched by psychoneuroimmunologists today—for precisely the reasons you have mentioned. It isn't logical to believe that the emotions make their registrations only on the downside. A moment ago I referred to Dr. Cannon's findings that the emotions can trigger biochemical reactions resulting in a substantial increase in the population of red blood cells.

You mean the human body can make its own blood transfusions under certain circumstances?

More accurately, the body can increase its own blood supply under circumstances of heightened purpose. But this is only one of a wide number of effects of the positive emotions now being studied. A moment or so ago, I referred to secretions produced by the brain.

You were talking about the body's own painkillers and about secretions that can combat infections and other forms of illness.

Medical researchers have been studying the possibility that attitudes can actually strengthen the body's immune system. All the body's systems are magnificent evidence of the way nature tries to help human beings get the most out of their own resources. The immune system, like the human brain to which it is connected, is high among the wonders of the universe. The system is beautifully designed to help meet the gravest threats that can confront a human being.

Begin with the fact that there are different kinds of immune cells to serve different purposes. Some of these cells are like sentries, roving throughout the body to search out intruders or invaders—disease microorganisms, for example. Immune cells are also capable of sounding the alarm that summons various kinds of disease-fighting cells to the danger sites. Do you recall my mention of interferons a moment ago?

Wasn't that the secretion activated by the brain that went to war against infections?

Also viruses. And, it is now believed, it even helps in the fight against cancer. There is evidence to show that interferons work with immune cells in combating various forms of disease, not excluding cancer.

How, exactly, does this work?

Some immune cells can embrace and crush cancer cells. There are immune cells that hook on to cancer cells, prying them open and depositing the body's own poison—or chemotherapy—directly into the cancer cells and killing them off, one by one.

I agree that this is a spectacular process. Such being the case, however, why does anyone ever die from cancer? Why don't the body's own cancer-fighting immune cells always do what they are supposed to do?

Actually, in the very great majority of cases, they do just that. During the course of a lifetime, most people, at one time or another, have cancer cells inside their bodies. But they never know it—precisely because the immune cells are dispatching them. But it sometimes happens that these cancer-fighting immune cells are weakened or depleted for one reason or another and cannot do their job—or the cancer cells are so potent that the immune system needs reinforcements.

You say that cancer cells are weakened or depleted. Why?

You will recall that we spoke of the drain represented by severe depression or worry or emotional fatigue—bereavement, for example. It has been established that such emotional wear and tear can actually destroy or weaken the cancer-fighting cells. Sometimes, of course, the body has to contend with an especially virulent cancer and a depleted immune system. It is hard to imagine a more melancholy combination.

Isn't there anything that can be done to restore a depleted immune system?

This brings us right back to the question you asked a moment ago. Everything involved in good health—a healthy emotional life, proper nutrition, a balanced lifestyle, adequate exercise—figures in the equation. As it concerns the emotional factor in that equation, some medical researchers are now discovering that the positive emotions—which you correctly identified as love, hope, will to live, purpose, determination, confidence, festivity, and good spirits—can be no less effective in bolstering the immune system than the negative emotions are in weakening it. It would be a serious mistake, however, to substitute psychological factors for competent medical care. Cancer is a powerful enemy. What is most desirable is a combination of forces in which we make ourselves the beneficiaries of the best that medical science has to offer and in which the full array of our own physical and mental resources are brought to bear. Medical science works best when the patient is panic-free and has full confidence in the physician and in himself or herself.

Does the immune system come into play only in preventing or combating illness?

The immune system is part of a total mechanism of response to challenge. When I spoke of the brain and the secretions at its command, I was referring not just to a disease-fighting mechanism but to a magnificent system for responding to challenge—whatever it might be. We are really talking here about the full activation of human potentiality. Toynbee, the eminent British historian, had a theory of challenge and response as the key to human progress. What is most fascinating about human beings is that it is impossible to think of any challenge that is beyond human capability.

It is difficult to imagine a more robust reason for a belief in a Deity than is represented by human endowments, especially human potentiality. Otherwise, we would have to attribute these wonders to happenstance or an accident—both of which are far more difficult to comprehend than the existence of a Great Design.

The significance of what we are talking about, of course, applies not just to the individual human being but to human beings collectively. The potentiality of the human species is the single most significant and exciting fact about human life. What would you say are the principal problems confronting the human species today?

First of all, of course, danger of nuclear war. Then hunger. Next, probably, human disease and the inadequacy of medical care for the overwhelming majority of human beings on earth. Then the deterioration of the conditions that support life—for example, the depletion of the rain forests, which supply such an important fraction of the world's need for oxygen. Also, of course, the effects of chemical dumping in the oceans, resulting in a gross reduction of plankton, which are oxygen producers, thus jeopardizing the ocean's chain of life—a condition seriously worsened by the predatory assault on the fish stocks of the world. I haven't even mentioned the use of the sky as an open sewer for radioactive materials, whether through accident or design, to say nothing of the increasing burden of sulfur dioxide and carbon monoxide. Do you want me to go on?

Your catalog of manmade catastrophes is full enough. But at least we know that we have capabilities and potentialities for correction and reversal.

Are you saying that these potentialities will automatically and magically assert themselves?

No, just that we need not accept an attitude of collective defeat toward our problems out of an imagined belief that they are far greater than we are. Just as the sense of depression, despair, or defeatism can impair individual health by depleting our immune systems, so collective negative attitudes can obstruct our potentialities in meeting our problems. These potentialities do not assert themselves automatically. We have to recognize the existence of the dangers before we can respond to them. We then have to decide on a course of correction. Finally, we have to commit ourselves to essential action.

The capability of human beings to meet any situation, however complex or precarious, is probably the most impressive fact in the cosmos. Unlike the planets, human beings have infinitely expandable capabilities that are inherent in biology, free will, intelligence, and spirit. There is no more awesome evidence of a Deity than that which exists in human potentiality.

In that case, are we to regard the fact that some human beings are born deformed or crippled or diseased as negative evidence of the existence of a Deity?

Thomas Jefferson and his colleagues struggled with inequalities in the human condition—represented by mental retardation, poverty, squalor, and disease—and concluded that these inequalities might be beyond philosophical comprehension but are not beyond care or correction. They recognized their responsibility to deal with injustices—whether political or social or biological. The Declaration of Independence does not assert that people are born with equal physical and mental endowments. What it says is that they must have equal access to political and social justice, the same right to freedom, the same right to seek out happiness in their own terms. The state doesn't create life. The state has the obligation to respect life, uphold it, and guarantee the freedoms and natural rights that come with the fact of birth.

All this I can understand. I can comprehend the political philosophy that holds that all human beings are created equal in terms of their natural rights. What I find difficult to understand is how we can reconcile the fact of basic inequality of birth with the concept of a just Deity.

You have identified one of the oldest and most persistent questions in theology and philosophy. Belief in God rests not just on the idea that God is all-powerful and all-wise, but also on the idea that God is infinitely fair, infinitely just, infinitely merciful. Could we believe in a Deity who was unfair, unjust, unmerciful?

No. I suppose that if God is not the source of justice and mercy, then a large part of the appeal of the Deity would be lost.

Precisely. One of the things that almost all religions have in common is the belief that God is the source of justice and fairness and mercy. Yet, as you say, nothing is more unjust than the uneven distribution of brainpower or ability to command one's destiny. Some human beings live only a few minutes or days; others become centenarians. Some human beings seem condemned to lifetimes of poverty, misery, squalor, disease, indignities. Can God be blamed for these deprivations? If so, then what happens to the concept of a just Deity? Some religions—in India, especially, where deprivation is almost a basic law of life—account for the disparity in the human condition by the belief that some people are paying for the sins of a past lifetime by their deprivation in this lifetime, but that they can earn their way into a more rewarding station in the next lifetime. In short, the processes of justice not only extend beyond one's lifetime but are built into a collective design.

I am still troubled by the natural disparities—at least, as they are perceived by the human mind. How does one reconcile the vast differences in natural endowments between a toad and a swan? Is it not possible to recognize a difference in function and beauty between one species and another? Is there no question of biological justice involved in the fact that some species, because of their intelligence and physical characteristics, are able to sustain themselves, while others are easily victimized and conquered. Between the worm and the human being, there is a wide range of natural endowments.

These questions are essential. We can also ask whether the worm is troubled by these limitations. Are animals conscious of the fact that they do not have the brainpower of human beings, or the opposing thumbs that enable them to make and use tools?

Assuming that animals do have this awareness, do they resent their station? If they lack the consciousness that enables them to contemplate their condition, what difference does it make?

Whether or not it makes a difference to the worm, our own senses can perceive vital differences. We like to speak of human uniqueness—by which we mean qualities and characteristics beyond those possessed by other species. When we do that, of course, we are also saying that God permits other creatures to be inferior.

I find it difficult to reconcile this fact with proof of God.

Some religions regard the inequality between species as being essential in God's design. Justice is represented by the fact that each creature is believed to take its turn at being everything else. In those religions, we take our turn at being a worm or a swan or an insect or a human being. In this way, we are all equally endowed in that we are expressions of the total cycle as part of a universal design. In this way, there is no inequality, no disparity—only ultimate justice. Some religions recognize a hierarchy among living creatures of which all beings eventually partake.

I can see how some people need to accept these formulations because of their own conditions.

Everything is explicable and comprehensible if all life is regarded as sequential as well as eternal, taking different forms, sometimes as rewards or punishments.

But what about biological or social injustice within the human species?

Here, too, since it is impossible to believe that God is unjust or unmerciful, the fact of squalor or deprivation or disease is not to be regarded as the ultimate condition. Consider the implications. The moment we separate a Supreme Being from justice, kindness, and mercy, he ceases being a deity and becomes something else— in some cultures, a devil. This defines the dilemma confronting human beings in their understanding of God. The belief in a merciful, kind, and just God conflicts with the evidence of natural inequality and natural justice—both within and outside the human species.

Very well, then, how do religions resolve these questions?

The questions are never fully resolved, but at least religions—some religions, that is—come to terms with the paradox by the way they think about themselves in relationship to God.

Can ways of thought actually make it possible to live with the paradox?

In most cases, what happens is that a rationale is created that enables human beings to regard inequality in intelligence, physical capacity, health, and conditions of living as part of the design.

Is this done by ignoring the evidence?

No. The conditions of life on earth cannot be separated from a large design. The test of a just God is not measured solely by what is apparent to the senses. Belief in a just Deity in those religions is sustained by recognizing and accepting reasons for the unevenness in the distribution of life's blessings. One might say that takes the form of balancing mechanisms.

Balancing mechanisms?

A way of making things come out even. If a person is deformed or disadvantaged in this lifetime, it is believed that divine justice will make it possible for that person to be properly endowed and advantaged in the next. Injustice is not forever. Also, disadvantages in this lifetime may be punishments for the sins of previous lifetimes. What is your impression of the Untouchables of India?

Just that they are relegated to the lowest levels of society.

Correct. But are you aware that the quintessential characteristic of the Untouchables is that they do not resent or protest their condition? The Untouchable may be deprived of all political and social rights; he may be grossly discriminated against—but he does not protest or ask for relief. In recent years, attempts have been made to correct this situation by preventing people from exploiting the passivity or acquiescence of the Untouchables. What confronts us, therefore, is the lack of desire of some groups to seek justice or equality for themselves. Paradoxically, this very belief in a just Deity has led the Untouchable to accept the injustice.

That would appear to be a contradiction in terms. Why would anyone regard a wretched life as a manifestation of divine justice?

Isn't it possible that this may be the only way to comprehend the hideous injustice in human affairs? The Untouchable is sustained by the belief that he is paying for the sins of a previous existence and that his acceptance of his present lot is both a necessary condition and a prelude to a better situation in his next life on earth. In this way, the belief that God distributes justice evenly is sustained. By accepting his lot, the Untouchable qualifies himself for a better life the next time around.

Surely such suffering cannot be regarded as part of a Great Design?

It is precisely the belief that God is fair that creates the philosophy of acceptance. The certainty that God cannot be anything but fair makes it necessary to attribute disparities and inequalities on earth to other causes—such as misdeeds or sins, whether in this lifetime or in previous ones.

The disparity between the Untouchables and those more fortunately situated is only one manifestation of injustice among human beings. The injustices human beings inflict on one another account for only a small portion of injustices on earth. As we recognized earlier, sickness, crippling, disfiguration, stunted mentality or stunted growth—all these have to be reconciled with the belief in an infinitely wise and just Supreme Being.

Hence the fact that in some cultures the cyclical nature of life is emphasized. The underprivileged and the oppressed have the hope of being elevated into a more rewarding life.

Somehow I find it difficult to acquiesce in the proposition that God sees to it that everything comes out even in the end. What counterbalance can there possibly be to the evil of Adolf Hitler? What "balancing mechanisms" can offset mass murder?

After Hitler, I suppose the main question is not just whether we can believe in God, but whether we can believe in man. It isn't as though Nazism came on the world without warning. We can't exempt ourselves from all responsibility. In any event, what is now important is that we have the ability, if we will use it, to learn from the evil of Hitlerism and to prevent it from recurring. We are not relieved of responsibility for enlarging the scope of justice on earth.

What about the assassination of John Kennedy or Robert Kennedy or Martin Luther King, Jr., or Mahatma Gandhi?

We can exhaust ourselves in the search for the meaning of evil on earth. The fact that it exists and recurs cannot be reconciled with any philosophy based on reason. But it is important to recognize that evil is not supreme in human affairs. We may never conquer it, but we are not without means to combat it. Nor are we relieved of the obligation to reduce injustice on earth. Belief in God need not rest on the ability of human beings to make a heaven on earth or to eradicate everything that denies or threatens truth and beauty and justice. The mere fact of life, and the inequalities of life, commands respect for belief in a Deity. There is also a surrounding infinity. The more we contemplate existence itself, the greater our respect for what is known, and even greater our respect for what remains to be known. The main advances of knowledge in our time are not so much in science and technology as they are in the growing knowledge of human potentiality. Nothing in the universe is more complicated, more majestic, or more mysterious than the reach of the human mind.

Everything you have been saying seems to emphasize the role of human beings in the universe.

Philosophy and religion converge in the consideration of human beings as creatures of the universe, rather than as members of a species totally limited in mobility of thought and body. If we can adjust our approaches on what are actually the intermediate questions or matters, it might be easier to deal with the ultimate ones. We have a tendency to superimpose God on a design; in fact, we tend to equate our speculations about infinity with God.

Is this wrong or bad?

It may be neither wrong nor bad. It may be merely irrelevant—at least in the sense that we may be looking in the wrong direction. Do you recall what we were saying earlier when we came to the conclusion that this universe of ours and everything in it may actually be contained in a space which, in the context of infinity, may be smaller than the smallest part of the atom?

Yes.

Then, having equated time and matter at what is generally regarded to be zero, we said it makes no difference so long as what happens inside the subatomic particle or zero takes place within reach of our own experience—or our own function and essence, or, to call it by its philosophical name, reality—reality being the manifestation of cause, effect, interaction, and, finally, consequences.

The main point, therefore, is that there has to be a something in "nothingness." The universal vacuum cannot complete itself. It cannot, because there is a rejection of absolute nothingness. It is not the enormousness or the scope or the grandeur of what results from the rejection of nothingness that is primarily significant here. What is most significant is that true nothingness is impossible. Infinity would swallow us up, but it cannot. Nothingness surrounds us, but it cannot claim us.

The proof of God, therefore, is in this rejection of nothingness. In this sense, God is even greater than we have imagined. Not even science can conceive of pure nothingness; pure nothingness nowhere exists. The universe may be only a particle, but it asserts itself, and the nothingness is kept from becoming absolute. Thus, the universe is a vital particle. And there are vital particles inside it, the most vital of which is man.

Haven't we always looked to grandeur for proof of God?

The true contemplation of God ought to proceed not out of manifest phenomena, but out of a void. This is the final test of spiritual substance. If our spirituality proceeds out of awe, it loses substance as soon as awe is dissolved. God emerges in fullest glory, not when made to sit astride infinity or when regarded as an architect of cosmic spectacles, but when contemplated as the Ultimate Force that prevents the cosmic void from becoming absolute.

Whether the Great Design of Creation exists within a microcosm or macrocosm is unimportant; what *is* important is that the vital particles inside it have order and purpose, and that they exist. And there is a place inside that order for man, for consciousness, for conscience, for love. This is what is important. We are not children of relativity. We are children of God. And we are brothers. And we enjoy or suffer the consequences of our ideas, our acts, our hopes, and our fears.

6

Consequentialism

We have been talking about a "higher" immortality in a way that ties all human beings together. We have found meaning in life, even though we agreed that it would be difficult to prove objectively that life is not an illusion. We have considered the relationship of human beings to the universe and to infinity. We have examined the proposition that life may abound in the universe, and some of its implications. And we have discussed human uniqueness in terms of our ability to define purpose and to achieve it.

Is there any name for what we have been talking about?

You might call it "consequentialism." By consequentialism, I am thinking of the whole sequence of ideas by which earlier in our discussion we attempted to relate each member of humanity through time to each other member—the living, the dead, and the unborn—and also to relate us all to the universal order. Our discussion has been concerned with the need for complete integration—integration of intellect, conscience, knowledge, intuition, feelings, and experience. Also, essential integration with the outside world. We recognize that progressive integration is a basic law of life. The development of the complex mechanism of a human being from a single cell is only one example. Similarly, each individual human being is only one part of a larger being or body that we call the human species. The challenge to the individual is to comprehend this oneness and then live it out.

But why would you call this consequentialism?

A moment ago, we said that the significance of reality was of lesser importance than the fact of life itself. For life is rich in its consequences. Consequences give reality to man's capacity to struggle between good and evil, nobility and venality, altruism and selfishness. A human being fashions his consequences as surely as he fashions his goods or his dwellings. Nothing that he says, thinks, or does is without its consequences. Just as there is no loss of basic energy in the universe, so no thought or action is without its effects, present or ultimate, seen or unseen, felt or unfelt. Reality is consequence. At every stop in life, we are coping with the consequences of ideas and actions, most of them long since forgotten. These consequences or effects are the unseen factors in individual life and the affairs of man; they are imponderables only in the sense that they are not directly identified. But they are no less vital than that which is explicit and accessible in human experience. In short, life is of consequence—literally so. Wisdom consists of the anticipation of consequences—and I remind you that consequences can be both good and bad. May I ask what has emerged from our discussion so far?

What I get out of it is my unpreparedness for dealing with such ideas.

Maybe that is why scientist-philosophers prefer equations and symbols in order to deal with the interaction of forces without at the same time defining them. Still, those who are not scientists must do the best they can with language. Now, what else would you say has emerged from our discussion?

In addition to the language barrier, I gather there is also some difficulty in making the necessary adjustments in our conventional thinking because most of our concepts are contained inside a frame of reference—in this case, a conventional frame of reference.

Would another way of putting it be that for all our lofty philosophical excursions, we are still earthbound? Aren't we overly fond, perhaps, of applying our concepts about size, direction, time, space, energy, to situations in which those concepts may be completely extraneous? We are measurement-minded. In fact, we have to be, because our plane of existence necessarily utilizes such concepts. Yet there is a larger plane on which those approaches may have no validity.

We have been talking, therefore, about barriers in the way of a fluent understanding of what we have been discussing. What about the subject of the discussion itself? Does any key fact emerge for you?

Yes. What I get out of this primarily, and I have no way of knowing if I am right, is that we have been looking in the wrong direction for proof of immortality itself, and that we may also have been looking in the wrong direction for possible answers to the mystery of reality—whether immediate reality or universal reality.

We have tried to throw our arms around infinity, and we have been left not with the universe in our arms but with a closed and empty circle. Hence, the more we know about the discernible and the theoretical universe, the more confused we become. Boundlessness or endlessness at first fascinates us, then appalls us. But I am interrupting. Please tell me what else emerged from our discussion.

The fact, of course, that human brotherhood is a reality.

Anything else?

We need not feel defeated or diminished by the fact that the greater our knowledge, the greater the ultimate mystery.

We have to continue to probe, to speculate, to try to fit things together. The eternal questions persist: How do we explain a universe without boundaries? Why, indeed, must there even be life, space, matter, time? Why must there be anything?

Are we any closer to the answers than when Socrates held his dialogues?

One wonders. But that is not what is mainly important. What is mainly important is that our natural endowments make it possible to ask ever deeper questions. There is spiritual and philosophical satisfaction in being able to conceive of the existence of ascending mysteries. The ultimate mystery increases with the right questions. We possess far more scientific and verifiable information about the universe than did previous generations. We have been able to correct fundamental errors in the old notions of the way the world was constructed. We know that there are billions upon billions of planets and stars in the universe, some of them probably very much like our own. We know much more than we ever did about the interaction of the universal forces. But all this enlarged knowledge serves mainly to enlarge the ultimate mystery: What is the secret of existence? The growth of science actually gives greater substance to the unknown.

Are you saying that that ultimate mystery will never be solved?

As to that, no one can say. We have increasingly clear ideas about the questions underlying the mysteries. What is most important here is that no one need fear that belief in a Deity will shrink as we increase our knowledge. The more we know, the greater our awareness of a Great Design.

Do you have articles of faith?

These are the articles of my faith:

I am a single cell in a body of five billion cells. The body is humankind.

I glory in the individuality of self, but my individuality does not separate me from my universal self—the oneness of man.

My memory is personal and finite, but my substance is boundless and infinite.

The portion of that substance that is mine was not devised; it was renewed. So long as the human bloodstream lives, I have life. Of this does my immortality consist.

I do not believe that humankind is an excrescence or a machine, or that the myriads of solar systems and galaxies in the universe lack order or sanction.

I may not embrace or command this universal order, but I can be at one with it, for I am of it.

I see no separation between the universal order and the moral order.

I believe that the expansion of knowledge makes for an expansion of faith, and the widening of the horizons of mind for a widening of belief. My reason nourishes my faith, and my faith, my reason.

I am diminished not by the growth of knowledge but by the denial of it.

I am not oppressed by, nor do I shrink before, the apparent boundaries in life or the lack of boundaries in the cosmos.

I cannot affirm God if I fail to affirm man. If I deny the oneness of man, I deny the oneness of God. Therefore, I affirm both. Without a belief in human unity, I am hungry and incomplete.

Human unity is the fulfillment of diversity. It is the harmony of opposites. It is a many-stranded texture, with color and depth.

The sense of human unity makes possible a reverence for life.

Reverence for life is more than solicitude or sensitivity for life. It is a sense of the whole, a capacity for inspired response, a respect for the intricate universe of individual life. It is the supreme awareness of awareness itself.

I am a single cell. My needs are individual, but they are not unique.

I am interlocked with other human beings in the consequences of our thoughts, feelings, actions.

Together, we share the quest for a society of the whole equal to our needs, a society in which we neither have to kill nor be killed, a society congenial to the full exercise of the creative intelligence, a society in which we need not live under our moral capacity, and in which justice has a life of its own.

Singly and together, we can live without dread and without helplessness.

We are single cells in a body of five billion cells. The body is humankind.